Tammy has an amazing way of finding humor in everyday life. As you read through her words, you see that hurt and discouragement can be powerless in the midst of true joy. As Tammy shows, sometimes one brave choice is all it takes to turn your life around.

—**Jon Acuff**, *New York Times Bestselling Author*

When I met Tam, I never would have guessed that she has gone through such traumatic, difficult experiences. Why? Because she's so full of life, joy, and fun. After getting to know her more, I have come to realize she oozes joy because she *chooses* joy. She's endured more painful situations than most anyone else I know, but she hasn't allowed that to make her a victim. Instead, she's chosen to be a victor. She serves as an inspiration to everyone she meets: you can have hope and healing after heartbreak.

—**Crystal Paine,** *Founder of MoneySavingMom and New York Times best-selling author of Say Goodbye to Survival Mode*

What if God truly can redeem all the parts of our story? What if He can leverage all of our hurts, pains, disappointments and bad choices to shine His light brighter? Do you believe that? Tammy Hodge doesn't just believe, she lives it. Through her compelling, honest and redemptive story she invites us to experience the God that makes all things new and works everything for our good and His glory.

—**Justin Davis** - *RefineUs Ministries, Co-Author of Beyond Ordinary: When a Good Marriage Just Isn't Good Enough*

I love Tam Hodge for writing this story, for being brave enough to dig into her heart and past and share those memories and dreams with us. This book is a sweet offering of thanks to the God who redeems all things.

—**Annie F. Downs**, *Author of Let's All Be Brave*

I'm so honored to support my dear friend Tam in the writing of her first book. Rarely have I known a person with such tenacity for hope, and I have no doubt that anyone who reads these pages will agree with me. I've had the privilege of hearing some of these stories over coffee, listening as she recalls the raw reality of a life that could have stolen her joy and devastated her family for generations. Instead, she chose (and continues to choose) the way ahead of her instead of the way behind. As a result, she has blessed her husband, her children, her friends, her readers, and most of all-her God. With unwavering commitment to truth, Tam has given us a breathtaking example of what can bloom from desert soil. I have no doubt you'll be moved by her heart, her words, her faith, and her ever-present sense of peace as you travel with her through the days that led her here. I'm incredibly proud to be a part of this exquisite offering. Well done, Tam.

—**Angie Smith**, *Best-Selling Author*

Choice is something that we all take for granted. We don't realize the gift it is until we feel like it is gone. In "And Now I Choose," Tam Hodge weaves a story of grace, hope, and truth, into a formula that leaves the reader with a massive choice - the choice to live or exist.

—**Carlos Whittaker**, *Author/Speaker*

And Now I Choose

Tam Hodge

Photography by Daniel C White
[**www.danielcwhitephotography.com**]

I dedicate this book to my dear friend, Sara Frankl, who showed us all what it looks like to truly Choose Joy. Thank you, sweet friend, for gracing this earth with such beauty, strength, and courage. I love you and miss you every day, Gitz. I'll see you soon.
Have some frozen Oreo's waiting for me.

—Tam

Contents

Part 1 – Choosing Survival

Part 2 – Choosing Freedom

Part 3 – Choose Joy

Foreword

I don't know any other way to say it than this: my friend Tam is a beautiful trophy of God's grace.

I've had the privilege of knowing Tam and her family for years now. I've watched God use her and her story to empower, encourage, and challenge countless people. I was so excited when I found out that she was pushing back against the fears that kept her from writing this book years ago. In this book, Tam brilliantly guides us through her story with a disarming transparency and authenticity that is rare in today's world.

I get the opportunity to serve alongside Tam's husband, Brent, at our church. One of the many "sayings" or "slogans" we've developed at the church we serve together is, "Everyone is welcome, because nobody is perfect, but anything is possible." And we really believe that.

We believe that no matter what you've done, where you've been, no matter how far away you feel from God today, we worship a God of open arms. A God who says, "Everyone is welcome."

Not only do we believe "everyone's welcome, because nobody's perfect," we're also relentlessly committed to the idea that "anything's possible." And I think you may be too. Perhaps it's why you picked up this book. You know that transformation in your life is possible. You know that healing is possible. Inside of you there is something that says there's more to life here on this earth. You long to become the man or woman God created you to be when He thought you into existence.

Have you ever noticed how most of us like to cheer

for the underdog? Most great stories have some kind of underdog theme. We love to believe in our core that every life makes a difference. And we are right. There is no one God can't use and no one whose brokenness is too broken for God.

We know this is true for our friends when we want to encourage them. Yet, when it comes to the places of our innermost sense of shame and regret, we often wonder if it is really true that God can work all things together for good for those who love Him.

This is why Tam's book is so brilliant. Over and over again her story will remind you that from the very moment humanity fell into sin, God's plan, God's passion, has been to redeem us and restore us to the life for which we are made. She reminds us that God is bigger than our history and more concerned with our destiny.

So as you dive into this book, I want to encourage you to "buckle up." You're about to go on an honest, hopeful, and exciting journey with Tam—one in which you will be blown away by the extraordinary things God has done in her life. But more importantly, when you finish this book, you'll be convinced God can do something extraordinary through you, as well.

Tam's story is really a story of God's love – His passionate and relentless pursuit of our hearts. Reading her story will remind you that God is in your story, in your life, drawing you closer to Him minute by minute.

—Pete Wilson
Pastor of Cross Point Church
Author of Plan B and Let Hope In

Prologue

Writing this book was not an easy task. It required rediscovering and then revealing some of my memories that seemed best forgotten. For years, I shied away from telling my story because I always had a picture in my head of women gathered in a room sharing their "testimony" with each of them "one upping" the other. That's not the person I wanted to be. It appeared to me that if I ignored the truth of my past life, somehow the truth would disappear, but it didn't. Why would someone want to listen to my story anyway? However, God had His plan and His time for me to share it with you, and I believe the time is now.

I could write endlessly about injustices done to me while growing up, and there were many. Abuses that happened to me should never have happened to any young girl. Although I was a victim then, I am not a victim now! It has been a long hard road to put the past where it belongs...in the past. Occasionally, a piece of yesteryear creeps into my thoughts, and while I reflect on what was then, I quickly rejoice over what is now.

I have so many memories. Many of them did not surface until well into my adulthood. They are memories that shed immediate light on certain behaviors or habits I had in that moment. Recalling pieces of my past has served to benefit me in several ways. When I think about some of the things I used to do and cringe about now, it only reminds me of the person I do not want to be today. Each time a part of my unpleasant past resurfaces, it only reaffirms the importance of aspiring to be the best parent, wife and friend I can be so the repetition of my behaviors stop, and the cycle is broken. I hope and pray this book reveals that you do not have to harbor anger and resentment, or carry guilt for poor choices you have made, or what people have done to you. Any injustice can be turned into a victory in your own life.

Your past does not have to own you. It has as much power over you as you allow it. My journey is one filled with heights and depths, mourning and celebration, sadness and joy. It is a journey I invite you to take hoping you might see a piece of yourself in me: that you can gain the courage to stand up and take captive the things that imprisoned you...that have prevented you from experiencing true joy and freedom. I have found that this source of hope only comes directly from God. As I allowed Him to reveal to me what He desired in my life, what He had intended for me all along, I began to taste His peace, and I wanted it to last forever. And, in my heart, I desire this peace for you, as well.

Part 1
Choosing Survival

It all starts somewhere.

The person you are today was formed by the experiences you've had in the past. Whether you are standing at a finished product or in the presence of your spouse of fifty years, it all had to start somewhere.

What we believe about family, love, and God is shaped through our experiences from the moment we are born. Here are some of the moments that shaped me...

Part 1, Chapter 1

A Drink of Water

A drink of water. That's all I wanted. I was very thirsty and had been patiently waiting for someone to help me...to be noticed, yet I would have to wait and sit quietly by myself. I knew not to bother anyone. But the more I played and waited, the thirstier I became until I couldn't stand it any longer.

After what felt like hours, I got up from the couch, where I had been sitting alone in the living room, and I slowly started down the long hallway toward my parents' bedroom. My big, relentless strides wilted to smaller, tinier steps the closer I got to their room. I grew more afraid of the noises that began escalating in volume. I paused, halfway down the hall, second-guessing my thirst. But my desire for a drink won out.

As I approached my mother and father's closed door all I could hear was Dad, screaming. Screaming so loud that his words were indiscernible. The sound of his voice at that volume was nothing like I had ever heard before. It was as though hot rocks were stuck in his throat. I'd never been so frightened in all my life.

Before I made a fist to knock on their door, I stood in the hallway waiting until the yelling stopped.

Knock. Knock.

The door remained closed. My father continued to scream. I made another fist and knocked a second time, a bit louder, less scared, and more determined for that glass of water.

Suddenly, I heard a loud crashing noise. I called for my Mama as my father swung open the door. I jumped and gasped for air. He just stood there, blood dripping from his fist that he had slammed into the very door I stood on the other side of, knocking. I looked down at my own fist. Oh, how different his and mine looked from each other's.

We locked eyes as he screamed to my Mama, "See what you made me do!" I froze. I couldn't answer. Nothing. What did I want again? Why had I knocked?

Staring fearfully into his eyes, I saw my Mama from the side, sitting on the edge of the bed, and I ran quickly past my father straight into her arms. He never moved. His breaths were deep and heavy. Drops of sweat were falling from his face and beads of blood still dripping from his hand.

Mama held me tight, and I was snuggled safely in her arms. I looked up at her and whispered very softly, "I'm so thirsty, Mama."

This is my first childhood memory. I was only three years old.

Part 1, Chapter 2
Find The Funny

The yelling, thumping, the sound of flesh being punched and smacked around was nothing new to me. It was an all too common, middle of the night, weekly ritual in our home. A custom I had no idea I shouldn't be accustomed to. What does a little girl know, right?

It's strange how things in life become our normal even when there is nothing normal about it. It is just a part of an ordinary life.

The quiet. Oh, the quiet of the mornings. In the eerily silent mornings that followed the night beatings I heard my Mama endure, one could feel the tension and fear in the early hours. It felt much safer to lay in bed, awake, but never opening my eyes, because in my mind's eye, I always expected to find the worst.

But this one dreary winter morning would soon prove to be very different. It became the day that would forever change my way of thinking. A day that altered the way in which I'd view each moment from then on.

Most mornings it took me quite a while to muster up enough courage to leave my bedroom. I never knew what I might find on the other side of my door. This was a common deterrent to my dashing out for a bowl of Frosted Flakes in which I often put two sugar cubes. These were the same cubes I would steal as a snack when my mama wasn't looking, or when the eyes on the back of her head were closed. That was a rare but celebrated, occurrence.

Eventually, I did make my way out of my fluffy pink twin bed that morning. Walking bit by bit to my door, I press my ear against it to listen for sounds, any sounds. I only wanted to hear my Mama's voice so I would know she was okay.

I place my tiny 8-year old hand on the doorknob, turn it and slowly pull it towards me. With just enough space to peep my head out, I brush my dark brown curls out of my eyes and stare down the hallway hoping to see Mama walk by. I wait, but see and hear nothing. And nothing was more troublesome than nothingness.

Taking a deep breath, I step out of my room. My heart begins to race. I never knew what I would find. Would Mama be sitting, crying, at the dining room table? Would there be laughing like nothing had gone on the night before? Would there even be anyone home? Would I be alone? Making my way down the hall, I know anything is possible. Oh, what is it about long, scary walks down hallways? When I finally make it to the kitchen, I do find my Mama, moving. A bit slowly, but she is moving. She has her back to me as I wait for her to notice that I'm standing behind her.

She finally turns around, pauses, and smiles. I look at her, pull my head back, somewhat perplexed at what I am seeing. Mama is wearing sunglasses. In the kitchen. In the morning. In the middle of winter. What? Why? Oh my God, my mama has finally flipped!

Still, having not said a word, she walks toward me and kneels down to my eye level. I, peering carefully through the lenses of her sunglasses, can see her swollen, black and blue and cut eyes. And my big, round hazel eyes begin filling up with tears. She reaches out, grabs firmly onto my shoulders and says this... "Tam, I have been looking for the perfect occasion to wear these sunglasses that I have had for months. I'd say today is a perfect day for that, wouldn't you?"

Still unsure of what is happening, I am silent. Mama continues on, speaking words that have never left my mind...

"Tammy, if there is one thing you do in life, because life will be hard, do this...Find The Funny! There will always be something to smile about. Make sure you find that something. Now, don't these glasses look great on me?"

When I think back, I remember her words, "If we can just find the funny, everything would be okay." I am sure she didn't understand that there was a kernel of truth in her words. I now know, however, that Mama was deceiving herself and avoiding the truth. She was trying to cope with a reality that wasn't funny at all for her or for us. But, still, I held on to it...

Part 1, Chapter 3
Don't Tell Your Mom

His eyes were very friendly. They had a sparkle in them. In fact, they smiled even when his mouth wasn't smiling. Not how I remember my dad's eyes at all. Although it had been many years since I had last seen my real dad I will never forget the look in his eyes when he yelled at my mother while shaking his dripping, bloody knuckles. But this new man, Danny, he was Mama's new boyfriend. Danny made us laugh. He had a goofy side to him. I'm pretty sure he was just an over-sized kid. He enjoyed taking us on little trips out of the blue. My brother and I loved those opportunities because they often meant getting pulled out of school early. What kid doesn't like that? Instant "Mama's new boyfriend" brownie points!

Mama seemed to like Danny a lot, too. She lit up every time he walked through the door. And it had been a long time since we'd seen her light up. She was happy. She really liked this one, so that made me happy too. I loved seeing Mama smile. It was one thing that made me feel safe for safe moments were treasured moments.

I can remember the afternoon when she got a phone call. Danny told her he'd be a little late for their date that evening. She didn't seem to mind. Danny arriving late was better than him not arriving at all. The child-like giddiness in her voice as she spoke to him on the phone made me happy. She would laugh and lovingly sigh, and I just sat and stared at her as I often did, admiring her beauty.

Though I was only 10 years old, I was already daydreaming about the day I would have those sorts of mushy, gooey-fun feelings, and long conversations. If I had ever wanted to know what it looked like to walk on a cloud, this would be the day of my revelation. With the phone to her ear and the coiled cord in her hand, Mama glided, back and forth across the room, happily unaware of her surroundings, lost in her very own moment of glee.

But, now with Danny having to be late for their date, this meant Mama had a few extra minutes to spare, and she used that time to chat with me. We didn't have a lot of long talks. It wasn't that we couldn't – we just didn't. But I knew when she came over to sit next to me on the couch that she had a purpose in mind.

"So, Tam, what do you think of Danny?"

Suddenly, I cannot breathe, unable to inhale or exhale, lungs paralyzed. I instantly forget why I was so happy for her just seconds earlier. What just moments before were feelings of safety and relief, immediately turn into feelings of fear and anxiety. And my thoughts quickly recall the events from the night before...

* * * * *

I had a love/hate relationship with sleeping alone in my mom's and my queen bed. On one hand, I loved it because I got to sprawl out and take every new cool place on the sheet. I'd cover every square inch of that mattress. From corner to corner, the whole thing was mine. Mine all mine. On the other hand, I didn't like being alone and hated when Mama had to work so much, especially late into the night. It didn't matter to me that my older brother slept on the couch in the same room. He'd sleep through having garden hoses shoved up each nostril turned on full blast.

This night was unquestionably an "I hate that Mama isn't here" night. I would have forfeited ever feeling another cool spot on my sheets in bed again if I could have escaped this night. Unfortunately that wasn't to be.

I wouldn't be alone in bed for long.

As I begin drifting off to sleep with my brother lightly snoring on the other side of the room, I hear the bedroom door slowly open. I can tell right away that it was not my Mama. She had a familiar entry. All her clanging jewelry sounded like a symphony as she walked toward the bedroom. Her perfume scent grew stronger as she approached the door. But not this night, there was no symphony of clanging jewelry. There was no scent of her, just a stranger entering our bedroom.

Heart racing. Feet sweating. Ears on high alert. I hear footsteps softly walking on the shag carpet, items being placed on top of the dresser, the whipping sound of a belt being removed from its pant loops, and the sense of someone slowly approaching me. The bed moves, and I feel the covers being gently, and quietly, pulled back.

"Tammy?" I hear softly whispered beside me. I hold my breath. It's Danny. Why is it Danny? What is he doing here? Where is my Mama? Why is he getting into my bed? Why are his clothes off? Why won't my brother wake up?

Pretending not to hear him, hoping he will go away, I do not move or respond. Ever so slightly I open one eye. The room is very dark. I can't see or hear a thing except for the sound of my brother snoring. And Danny is lying next to me.

He lies there for a minute then puts his hand on my right hand. He rests it there for a few moments. His hand is warm and clammy. At this point, my heart is beating so violently it begins hurting my chest; pounding so hard I am sure it is jolting my entire body. Along with my panicky breathing, I am scared he may know that I'm awake. I pretend to sleep and try not to imagine what may happen next. I just keep hoping he will move and leave me alone. But mostly, I just want my Mama to come home.

Then it happened. He gripped my hand with his, brought it towards him, and placed it exactly where he wanted. Never loosening his forced hold on my 10 year-old little hand, he whispered, "Don't tell your mom."

* * * * *

"Tam? What do you think of Danny?"

Trying hard to get the emotions and fears from the night before out of my mind, I finally answer her...

"He's a nice man, Mama. I like him."

That evening I learned that this had to be my secret.

Part 1, Chapter 4

I Love You

One dish…that's all it was. One drinking glass left unwashed after my kitchen chores were done. I wasn't even out of the kitchen before he had walked in and noticed it before I did. I caught his stare turning toward the dirty glass, and I quickly followed with my own eyes that were already filling with tears. I knew instantly what my punishment would be, or so I thought!

I was used to his beatings and other physical assaults. They never surprised me. They always hurt in some form, but no longer startled me. Though, I certainly wasn't counting on a "spanking" this afternoon. I mean, I was just washing the dishes and daydreaming of Chancey Moore and wondering if I should invite him to my 13th birthday party. I did, after all, bring a pair of his pants home one day so I could dye them. I wanted them to match for a school performance that we both had leading roles in. I might have slept with said pants that night, too. Maybe. Nevertheless, that made us close, right? Or perhaps that just made me as creepy as it appears I am now that I'm writing all this out. Shish, Tam! But he was very cute, and completely unaware of my presence. Very cute. And I had his pants.

Back to the dishes. Walking home from school that

day, I had already planned on doing my chores first so I could get to my homework to finish in time for dinner. Mama had just taken on another job, but was going to be home and cook a meal that evening. She's the best cook! Country cooking queen, that lady. The house was quiet when I walked in. I thought I was the only one home. My brother was in high school at the time and got home much later than I did. So for Danny to walk in after I thought I was done was very upsetting.

"Tam, what is that?" he asked while he pointed to the dirty glass on the counter behind the sink.

"It is a glass," I responded with a shaky whisper.

"And you were just going to leave without washing it?"

"I'm sorry, I didn't notice it until right now. I'll wash it right away."

"No, don't bother. It is too late."

He walked over to me and gently grabbed my arm, pulling me toward the dining room table and chairs. His blue eyes sparkled as if he were full of joy.

"Bend over the back of the chair, Tammy."

I know not to say a word. Just do.

The sound of his belt swooshes out of his belt loops. An all too familiar sound.

"Take off your pants and underwear. You really deserve to feel this one."

For the next half an hour, half naked, I leaned over the back of the very chair where mom later would sit for dinner, and I take a beating from his belt, buckle, and occasionally his hands. He paces back and forth in between hits and reassures me that he is only doing this because he loves me.

Then just like that, he is done. He puts his belt back on and walks out of the kitchen, leaving me there bent over the chair, welted, bleeding, crying, and humiliated to my core. Due to the pain and blood from the hits, I am unable to pull my pants back up. Still half naked, I walk across the house and down the long hallway to my bedroom. Danny was nowhere in sight. I frantically remove my comforter from my bed and fold it in thirds. I open my closet door and lay the comforter down inside on the floor. I remove my favorite picture of my mama from the frame sitting on my nightstand. I step into my closet and close the sliding door behind me, leaving it slightly cracked for more light. I lie down on the blanket, take the gum out of my mouth and use it to stick my mama's picture up on the wall right where I lay my head. And I stare at it. And I cry. I talk to her picture. I tell her that I will never let this happen to my daughter. Ever. And I beg her to come home.

I realized something very monumental at that moment, too. I couldn't possibly be the only girl that has ever been through this. I wondered how many other girls just got a colossal beating? Strangely, that comforted me. The idea that another 12-year-old was hurting at the same time, sad as it may be, soothed my fear, my pain. For the first time, I didn't feel alone.

Knock. Knock.

(Silence)

I say nothing.

"Tam?" It's Danny.

"Oh, please be done, please no more," I silently cried in my head.

"Where are you?"

"In the closet. I need the dark to nap." Oh, he is never going to fall for that!

"Oh, OK. I love you, Tammy."

(Pause)

"I said I love you, Tammy."

(Silence)

"I love you, too."

Part 1, Chapter 5

I Asked For It

We were on the run again and rightfully so. Mama was put in danger on many occasions, and this time was no exception to the norm. I was barely in junior high. My brother was a freshman, and our baby sister was still in diapers. The run, this time, was back to California from Alabama.

We knew it was coming. She prepped us earlier in the day. We were told to fit as many clothes as possible into a paper shopping bag, and that was it. Not one more personal item could go with us. I skirted off to my room as soon as dinner was done. Sitting on the edge of my bed, I looked around at what little I had, and I began to cry.

Just a few months prior, we left California for Alabama with the very man Mama is now running away from. But I sure do remember how excited she was to move to Alabama in the first place. I can tell she wanted to start over with new people and new surroundings. We lived with his family for several weeks until we found a place of our own. This house was on a lot of land that was lopsided, the house, not the land. The kitchen was huge and slanting. I'm not kidding. We would put my baby sister in her walker and watch her roll from one end of the kitchen to the other without her even trying. Her feet couldn't even touch the floor when she sat in the walker. We'd find her all over the house! This place wasn't worth much since it had an uneven foundation, garden snakes, (not in the garden but hiding in the house) and a wasp nest inside my room. I suppose it wasn't that bad.

The afternoon of the day we made our run back to California I was given the chore of separating the garbage into "burn piles" and "doesn't burn piles." Well, being a Southern California city grown girl, I had no clue what burned and what didn't. And the fact that Mama's boyfriend stood close by, inspecting my work, did not help my nerves and ability to figure it out without wanting to pee on myself from the fear of his nearby presence. I knew all too well the wrath that would take place if I messed this up. And, I messed it up. I asked a stupid question. Shaking, holding a thin metal grate in my hand, I asked him, "Does this burn?"

"Tam!" I yell at myself in my head. Before I completed the question, I knew it couldn't possibly burn. Why did I ask? Why do I always ask for it?

There I stood, holding out the metal piece of garbage, waiting for his answer. His eyes grew angry, and his top lip quivered as he reached out and tore it from my hand. "Does it look as though this will burn, Tammy?"

"No sir. I'm sorry."

And with that he threw it back at me, telling me how stupid I was. He threw it so hard and fast I couldn't catch it. But it caught me. It sliced my arm open on its way to lodging itself into my stomach. To this day I have scars in both places from that moment.

Seven hours later he is off with his buddies and we are frantically packing our car as full as possible with the things that were most valuable to us. My Mama, older brother, baby sister, and I all climb into the front seat of our Ford Torino to begin our journey back out West where we had garbage men who were paid to know what burned and what didn't.

Part 1, Chapter 6
Running On Empty

I know what hell feels like. It feels like four people crammed into the front, vinyl, bench seat of a Ford Torino in the middle of the hottest time of summer. My baby sister's poopy diapers, my teen brother's smelly armpits, my greasy hair, and Mama's cigarettes...hell. The car didn't have air conditioning, which meant the rolled down windows provided humid-smelly-hell...reserved only for the bravest of souls, of course.

These were the days, early 1980s, when you didn't have to wear a seatbelt, which was great for the baby because she was being breast-fed. Yah, and she didn't have a car seat. She spent most of the time eating on Mama's lap while she drove. I sat in the middle, and brother had the window seat. Behind us was the backseat full of everything we had left in life: a few clothes, several baby items, a small filing cabinet, two blankets, one pillow, and a Styrofoam cooler with cans of Coke in it. That was it. Our lives, in one backseat.

We had driven through the first night without sleeping. We were running on fear and adrenaline.

Although Mama always appeared to be so cool about things like this, I knew she was scared. She had to be. During the first day of driving, it was beginning to get intense. The heat, the crowdedness of being squished together on one seat, the reality setting in for each of us, the long, flat road ahead. So much to take in. So much time forced to having to take it in. Not wanting to take any of it in. So, we never spoke of it. We laughed. We told funny stories. We sang. We made up songs. We escaped while escaping.

After what seemed to be eleventeen hundred hours, the first full driving day came to an end. Mama pulled into a gas station/mini-mart. She gave my brother and me a few dollars to get some snacks for dinner while she and the baby washed up in the gas station bathroom.

It was late and super dark - eerily dark. I felt safe with my brother, though. He didn't express much emotion and certainly didn't appear to like me, but I knew he did. I knew he was watching out for me.

"Tam? What do you want for dinner?" He asked.

Slowly waltzing in the mini-mart aisles, pretending I was Wonder Woman (I always wanted to be her) and looking over my shoulder for bad guys, my eyes bolted to a pack of shiny black mini donuts. The sheen demanded my attention. There was a heavenly glow about them, and they would be mine.

"That! I'm having that for dinner," I answered.

"Well, all right, and a Slurpee?"

I wasn't dumb. I knew I needed to balance my food out with a beverage.

"Yes! A Slurpee!"

We made our dinner purchase and headed back to the car where we found Mama and baby sister sleeping in the front seat. Mama's short frame fit perfectly from one end of the seat to the other while the baby was tucked safely in her arms. Brother grabbed one of the two blankets from the back seat and covered them up and draped the remaining one over his shoulder and placed it on the hood of the vehicle.

"Hey, Tam! (Sitting and tapping his hand on the

hood of the car) Hop on up here and let's eat our dinner."

Loving that my brother actually wanted me to sit next to him, on purpose, I hopped right on up by him. He handed me my "oh-so healthy" dinner, and we dined together. He asked how the cut on my arm and hole in my stomach were feeling. I showed him my arm, he moaned, and then looked away. We quickly switched topics and began talking about how excited we were about going back to California. We missed our home, our family, and friends. I missed having a bedroom that didn't have a wasp's nest in it.

Eventually, we got tired enough and knew we needed to try and sleep. There were only a few cars in the parking lot. Occasionally a vehicle would pull in for gas, but it was mostly calm and quiet. Brother took the right side of the car's hood, and I took the left. He placed the blanket on us both, and we pretended it was all perfectly normal.

"Night, Tam."

"Night. Thanks for dinner."

Suddenly, squealing tires, laughter, and yelling abruptly awaken us. Brother sits up quickly and looks around. I wait for his reaction before I move. He lies back down and locks eyes with me, and I know not to move. Then, before we know it, a small pickup truck, with a few young men in the back, pulled up to our makeshift bed, grabbed our blanket, and sped off with it.

"At least they didn't hurt us," brother said. And with that, we laid back down and waited out the rest of the night. It's like it didn't even faze us. Or, we pretended it didn't.

After what seemed like 100 hours of waiting for daylight, morning finally came. Mama and baby got out of the car, and the first thing shouted from Mama's mouth, "Where's your blanket?"

I looked at my brother with huge eyes as he calmly said to her, "Oh, we gave it to someone who didn't have one."

My brother, not wanting to hurt or worry Mama, lied. He chose to lie to protect her heart, knowing full well she already hated what she was putting us through. This was our reality with miles and miles yet to go.

Part 1, Chapter 7

Me? A Model?

The day began as usual. A typical quiet morning as my mom and two younger sisters slept, and my brother and I got ready for school, packing our lunches, eating our breakfast, and managing not to wake anyone with our incessant bickering. It's a miracle we ever made it to school at all!

The walk to school was always my favorite part of the day. Living just a couple miles from the beach, there was an unmistakable uniqueness to the morning air. It was crisp, fresh, and smelled like smiles. I love the ocean. I love standing on its edge. The grandeur of the sea and the power of its waves make me feel so small, and yet, brave at the same time. Even though I had not given any attention to God then, I always felt there was something more to life when I'd walk the shoreline. The endless grains of sand and water spilling over the side of the earth, crashing waves so loud they'd shake your core, there just had to be something more behind it all. The walk to school took me just a bit farther from the shoreline, but the smell of the salty air and the sounds of seagulls circling above were constant reminders that I was just minutes away from where I felt courageously small.

My route to school was pretty much a straight shot. I didn't have to think a lot about where I was walking, which allowed my mind to drift off quickly. Most of my morning commutes would find me daydreaming about the life I might have someday. I'd be happily married with jovial, energetic, and obedient children running around a white picket fence in the front yard as their puppy chased them ferociously. At the same time, I would be dodging my lovely husband's car pulling into the toy-strewn driveway after a long hard day's work at his very well paying job.

Well, those were some of the only moments of escape from my reality. Oh, how I had longed for an extended walk to school. I desperately wanted to stay in my imaginary world all day. Sadly, the second I stepped foot on campus, reality would punch me straight in the face. Typically, it started out with fellow students making fun of how I smelled. It wasn't that I had poor hygiene, not at all. It was the effects of living in a house full of smokers. It didn't matter how many times I shampooed my hair that morning, or how much Navy perfume I sprayed on my clothes, there was no ridding myself of that heavy cigarette stench.

Then the attention would turn to my outfit for the day, which looked strangely similar to the outfit I wore the day before. I had very few clothes so I'd attempt to mix-and-match as I was able. But there were those few kids who were hell bent on keeping a "What is Tam wearing today again?" log and were sure to let me know of my repetitive fashion offense. It didn't bother me all that much until the day my World Civilization teacher commented on my clothes. During the third period, I sat in the front row in clothes I had already worn that week. Cowering in my long white skirt with a large floral print on it (don't judge) he walked up and down the rows and stopped beside me and said, out loud, "You really like that skirt, don't you?"

Right now, you might be going through the feelings I had in that moment: churning stomach, temperature rising, beads of sweat forming on my brow, complete and total humiliation. I was mortified. And the sounds of laughter from rows behind me certainly did not help the situation. That was the longest 52-minute class ever. I just wanted to walk out and never return. But I did return. Only this time my skirt would be different. I went home that day and made my floral, denim monstrosity (oh, yes, it was denim), a mini-monstrosity denim skirt. I cut that negativity off at the knee! Take that you clothes haters.

My one highlight at school was being with my best friend, Donna. To this day, I have no idea why she hung around with me. She was beautiful, thin, fashionable, and popular. Everyone always told her she should be a model. What I loved most about her was that none of it ever went to her head. I may not have had a bunch of cool clothes, spending money or popularity as she had, but we still had a connection. We are friends to this day.

During our lunch break, Donna asked me to go with her that evening to an appointment she had in the Valley at a modeling agency. Not surprised that she'd have this kind of gig and not wanting to ruin her chances by walking in with her, but wanting so badly to do something away from home, I immediately agreed to go along. My mom liked Donna, so she allowed me to go with her. Right after school we headed off to the modeling agency.

"You know, you have very pretty features," the agent said, "and you have good height for your age. Have you ever considered modeling?"

I'm sure my blank, stunned look resembled nothing of beauty. "Who? Me?"

Donna is standing off to the side with a big folder in her hands; smiling as she nods toward me. I stand up. I had been sitting for almost an hour in the waiting room while the BFF met with an agent. I felt so out of place. All the pictures hanging on the walls around me were filled with hopes, dreams, futures, and eating disorders...well, I wasn't thinking eating disorders then, but let's be honest. These girls were stunning and poised. I imagined they all came from perfect homes with perfect parents and had swatch watches in every color. I wasn't like any of them.

"Tam, meet my agent!" Donna said, once again trying to get me to stand up. I hopped up and gave Mr. Agent my firmest handshake and said, "Hey." Yes, I literally said hey.

"Would you be willing to come back in a few weeks and talk to a couple of our people?"

Never having been coached to maintain a decent face while stuck in a dramatic pause, I awkwardly stared at him with what must have looked like a mashed up face of Jason and one of his victims from the movie Friday the 13th.

"Um, like, for sure!" Remember, we were in the Valley, and we had to play the role. Next thing I remember, Donna and I were on our way back home giddier than two high school girls who had just left a modeling agency!

Part 1, Chapter 8

Who Said You Were Pretty?

Nothing could ruin our moment...blasting the best tunes of 1987 in our car traveling on our way home from the modeling agency while laughing endlessly in nervous excitement!

"You're a model!"

"No, YOU'RE a model!"

Well, we were model somethings, and we were on top of the world!

It was about a 45-minute drive home from Agoura Hills. Our enthusiasm never let up. Not only were we teenage girls, but naturally everything was to be responded to with a very high-pitched squeal. It's also a teen girl's nature to do a lot of clapping. So, yes, there was squealing and clapping in abundance. Oh my! We must have looked like sea otters. Finally, we arrived at my cul-de-sac. We looped around the court to the front of my house, reluctantly turned down our favorite Berlin song on the radio, promised to call each other in the morning, shared a BFF hug and one more squeal for good measure. And with that, Donna drove off, and I bounced excitedly up my front walkway.

With the sound of our favorite song being turned back up as the car drove away, I opened the front door to my house. It was a little late, so I was unsure if anyone would be awake. I walked past the stairs straight ahead to the dining room, aka, the Big Tangerine. Every surface of this room, including the attached kitchen, was painted bright tangerine, on purpose, by my mother...on purpose. There were houseplants everywhere hanging from the ceiling, in big pots, in the corners, sitting on shelves, and in the middle of the table. And all their green leaves accentuated those orange walls. It was a cheery room on one hand and quite offensive on the other.

In the middle sat a large, octagon-shaped table. I couldn't tell you what the table was made of because it was always covered with a vinyl tablecloth. Mom had a flare for thematic living, so each tablecloth coincided with seasons and holidays. Basically, it was a very busy room, filled with lots of stuff, cigarette smoke and, typically, lots of people because it was the hub of the house.

But not on this night. The closer I got to the big tangerine room, I saw my mom coming into view from the right. She was sitting alone at the table, just her, a drink, a cigarette, and an ashtray. No country music playing in the background, which was very unusual. The room was eerily quiet. Quite a shock to my jovial self just before I bounced into the house.

She looks slowly up at me, but says nothing. I walk in, make my way to the table, pull out the large swivel chair, and sit directly across from her. My heart is beating so fast! Not because the atmosphere is scaring me, but because I just had the best night of my life. I was really hoping she'd ask me about it! I couldn't wait to tell her what the man said at the Modeling Agency.

"How did it go, Tam," she asked in a monotone voice, seemingly uninterested, just doing her motherly duty. I didn't care. I took the opportunity to blurt it out all at once, in one long improper sentence.

"Mom, they want me to come back...ME! They said they'd like me to talk to an agent. He said I was tall, and had good structure. What does that mean? My eyes aren't uneven. My ears are, but they can work with that. My hair style is all wrong, but they can work with that, too, and they want me back in two weeks!"

With bated breath and eyes bigger than a full moon, I waited for mom to say something. She took in a half committed breath, peeled her arm off the vinyl tablecloth as she lifted her hand to her mouth to take another drag of her cigarette. She stared back at me and blinked at a snail's pace and asked me one question...

"Who ever said you were pretty anyway?"

Our eyes are locked in blank stares. My chest is pounding, my heart is in visceral pain, and my eyes are working their hardest to reject the tears that are forcing their way over the edge.

"Nobody, mom. Nobody." My tears won. There was no stopping them. In fact, my entire body begins to cry.

"Tam, just go to your room."

And just like that my excitement instantly turns into excruciating pain...pain at the core level. If I could draw a picture of this pain, it would be the darkest of dark at the center and jagged, sharp, life-piercing daggers at its edge. It is a pain I would wish on no one. Ever. Under any circumstance.

I swivel my chair to the right, stand up and walk up to my room. Mom didn't say another word...at that moment.

The very one who always pushed me to look on the bright side of life just shattered all its lights. There was no bright anything for me to find. All I hoped was that Mom would believe in me, to be excited with me, to encourage me to take a risk, to squeal and clap with me. I thought she would ask me a lot of questions about the trip, the agency, and the gentleman who wanted me to come back. But, instead, she asked me only one question, "Who ever said you were pretty anyway?" Not quite what I was expecting.

Part 1, Chapter 9
I Don't Like You Anymore

It's so hard to be happy when you've been hurt. I mentioned before that my mom always told me to find the funny in life, even in the worst of times. And there were a lot of "worst of times" in our lives, so I had a bunch of practice. In this moment, however, I tried so hard to find a funny, any funny, but I just couldn't.

Sitting on the edge of my bed, with my head in my hands, sobbing uncontrollably, all I can hear are my mom's words, "Who ever said you were pretty anyway?" Suddenly, mom storms in. She rarely got physical with me. The few times she did were doozies, but it wasn't spankings I feared from mom...it was rejection. If I had to choose to begin every morning with a colossal beating in place of ever having to feel rejected for even a nanosecond, I would take the colossal beating every single day...without hesitation. All I wanted in life was for my mom to notice me. I longed for her to walk alongside me and encourage me in my strengths - to ask me questions about my interests - to tell me she was proud of me. To this day, I thrive on words of affirmation. Perhaps that's just due to not experiencing them much as a child.

When she flung my bedroom door open, I jumped from one side of my bed to the other as she said three things to me:

"Call your dad."

"Get out of my house."

"I don't like you anymore."

She turns around and leaves.

I stand and back up against my bedroom wall, slowly slide down it in tears, ending up in a pile on the bedroom floor. Hunched over, sobbing, I realize I can't call my dad. I don't know where he is...again! So I call my best friend Donna, who calls my boyfriend, who immediately rushes to pick me up. I didn't sneak out. I just threw some clothes and necessities in a bag and waited for him to arrive, and I walked out. That was it; my last night at home. At the tender age of 16, I am now on my own and off to live with my boyfriend...not my choice.

* * * * * * *

Wow, this is awkward. But kind of cool. But mostly awkward. I just woke up in my boyfriend's bed, and he is beside me. Let's be honest, when you were a teen, you always dreamt about being an adult and on your own, right? Suddenly, I was. Even so, it didn't feel quite as fabulous as it did in my daydreams. It felt unnatural and scary.

I take a very deep, long breath and rub my eyes for an abnormal length of time. I am trying to avoid having to acknowledge that I am not in my own bed; rather, I am at my boyfriend's home in his bed. And he is next to me, asleep. I sit up quickly then fall back down onto my...I mean his...pillow and lay still, mannequin style still. My eyes are wide open and moving quickly back and forth, scouring his room, as my memories from the night before attempt to put all the pieces together.

Ah, yes... "Who said you were pretty? I don't like you anymore. Get out of my house." Three small sentences that would forever change my life. It all came flooding over me like a million unwanted bee stings.

He begins to stir. He rustles around and kicks his legs out from under the blankets. He turns to his left side and slowly opens his eyes. They connect with mine. Whoa. He doesn't look as cute as he usually does when I first see him in the morning. I mean, I've never seen him before 2nd period. That hair. Interesting. So guys really do spend time on their hair. Clearly, they must because I have never seen his hair look quite like this.

We share an awkward locked-eyes silence for a few seconds then say... "Hi."

And that was it. We hopped out of bed and got ready for school. I kid you not. It was as though this had been our normal all of our lives. We pretended this was how it was supposed to be. Yes, we talked about what happened the night before, but it was all too easy for us to step into this faux "playing house" mode. And we did it well. We did it all very well.

However, it wasn't long before the powers that be at my high school got an ear full of what had happened. It was during my third period science class when I was called to the principal's office. Ok, up until that moment, I had been called many things in my 16 years, but I had never been called to the principal's office! This was a new one for me. Walking on very shaky legs to unfamiliar territory, I arrive on the other side of the principal's office door. With a pink slip in hand, I knock. How horribly familiar this felt to my first memory when I knocked on my parents' door, and my father opened it with bloody hands. Again, I feared what was waiting for me on the other side. I stand there, shaking, sweating, and waiting.

"Come in!" All I really wanted to do was turn and run. That's all I've ever wanted to do.

I slowly turn the doorknob and push the door open. Peering my head around I see my principal. He always reminded me of Colonel Sanders. He walked the hallways a lot in between classes. He spent time with the students during lunch hour. He was like the campus grandpa. Until this day, however, my shy self had never spoken to him, though I had always wanted to. He sat behind his large, mahogany desk. His silver hair and bifocals rested on his crow's feet and laugh lines. I step into his office, and he smiles back at me. For the first time since I had been kicked out of my house, I felt safe.

"Please, take a chair, Tam. It has come to my attention that you've come across some hard times. How are you doing?"

Instantly tears begin to flow. Ugly crying tears. Billions of them. And I tell him my story…

Before I know it, two other people are called into the room, and they are all on speakerphone with Child Protective Services and my mother. It all happened so fast! My nails are digging into the arms of the leather chair as I listen in. There is a lot of talk about abuse, molestation, neglect, legalities, and truancy. I am crying in the background as I hear my mother nonchalantly dismiss the severity of the moment. Mr. Principal finally asks her, "What would you like to do?"

"Tell her she can come pick up her things after school today."

Dial tone…

Mr. Principal asks the others to step out of the office. He stands up slowly and walks from behind his desk toward me and sits down to my left.

"Tam. I want you to go get your things now. I want you to take my number. I know where you are staying. I know your boyfriend's mother…you'll be safe there. You can call me any time you want to. Do you understand what I'm telling you?"

I knew what he was communicating to me at that moment. I knew that he knew I would be better off leaving my home to go live with my boyfriend and his mother.

He never touched me. He didn't reach out to hold

my hand or hug me. Thinking back now, I respect him deeply for that. He understood. I was dismissed and I walked out of his office in tears. Passing secretaries, janitors, students, trying to hide my face, hide my fear, and hide the sadness...I walk back to class.

Having to wait until the next day, a fellow classmate offered to drive me to my house after school to pick up my belongings. My mother knew I was coming, and I was a nervous wreck the whole way there. I didn't want to face her. All I can think about was the sound of her voice on the speakerphone from the day before. I knew mom was furious over all the details Child Protective Services had shared with her. Right or wrong – no parent wants to hear that their child has been abused under their watch.

My friend and I turn left onto the cul-de-sac in which I lived. She swoops her car around and parks across the street from my house. Very reluctantly, I step out of the car. I stand by the door and try to calm my breathing. My chest hurts from the intense pounding from my heart. I take a step, and like every child is taught to do, I look both ways before crossing the street toward my front yard. Pausing at the sidewalk in front of my house, I can see through the wrought iron screen door into the living room. I can also make out a figure walking toward the door...it's my mother. I freeze and stand motionless on the sidewalk, I watch as she opens the screen door, holding a battered box in her arms.

"So, they tell me one of my boyfriends molested you?"

Frozen in fear, I say nothing.

"You probably liked it, Tam. Here. Here's your stuff."

She dropped the box on the doorstep and turned back into the house. And that was it.

"Tam! Just go get the box!" My friend yells at me from the car across the street. It's all I can do just to breathe.

I probably liked it? How could those words have come

out of her mouth?

I take a step forward off the sidewalk toward my mother's front door. Humiliated, I reach the doorstep and the box. Hoping she doesn't come back out as I try to gather enough strength to pick up the box. I bend down and grab it with my weakened arms as tears soak the folded, over-lapping cardboard tops that have secured it shut. The box is falling apart at the bottom. I cup my hands under the broken corners to keep things from escaping. I began walking back toward the sidewalk, across the street to the car. Items begin falling out through the bottom of this tattered box that I can barely hold on to as I am trying to rescue my 16 years of memories as they drop to the ground. The box is falling apart. I'm falling apart. Everything is falling apart. My life is no better than this tattered box filled with all I own.

This is my tattered life.

Part 1, Chapter 10
The Longest Walk

Many days, the crashing waves were my only friends. I'd sit on the shore and reveal my heart, pour out my fears, and let my falling tears kiss the whitewater swirling around my feet. As the ocean water crashed around me like a hug from something or someone much bigger than me, I momentarily chose to escape my life, a life without direction, a life full of unanswered questions and uncertainty.

At this time, I am still living with my boyfriend in his mother's home. I'd been with them since the end of March that same year. My boyfriend and I played house as so many misplaced teenagers did then, and sadly still do. It was like a craze; the youth living like adults. Yet we were still kids working hard at getting homework completed, fighting for our pictures in the yearbook, and planning sleepovers.

I remember the last week of school when it was all I could do to make it to class each morning. I came down with a dreadful flu bug, a relentless flu. One that went on long enough that a friend of mine finally suggested I see a doctor so that I would feel better for our "School's Out!" party. My boyfriend was oblivious to what I was going through. He was preoccupied with his friends and surfing. Never mind that I had already skipped two menstrual cycles, I was adamant this was the nastiest flu ever to hit my hometown, and it just happened to hit me! Eventually, a girlfriend, suggesting I might be pregnant, convinced me to call the Medical Clinic. The next morning, I made the phone call and got an appointment right away.

I couldn't even drive myself there because I didn't have a license or a car. My friend wasn't available, so my boyfriend bitterly put his surfing aside and drove me to the clinic. When we walked through the clinic's door that day, there was not one empty seat to be found. It was your average-looking doctor's office waiting area, but it overflowed with mostly young girls, the majority of them alone. I had never seen anything like it before.

We found a place to stand until two seats were available. We sat there for what seemed like hours. Fortunately, for me, I'm a people watcher. I like to believe I can accurately guess what one might be thinking. It was something to occupy my time and thoughts.

So naturally, I had all these girls pegged. I knew all of their stories. I wrote all their biographies in my mind while attaching to each girl their stories of sadness, neglect, and poor choices. One by one they were called to the back of the clinic, leaving me to shift my focus onto someone else sitting in that waiting room.

I remember how you had to exit the building by coming back through the front office and waiting room area. However, just a few of the girls ever made their way back through the front while a few of the others I never saw again. Still, I watched plenty of them pass me by, weeping, frightened, speechless, and leaving the clinic alone. I definitely became a bit anxious about my name being called. The idea that I might have had the longest flu in history became a welcomed theory. I was beginning to feel the fear.

Then it happened...my name was called.

The way they called your name wasn't very inviting. You know how you wait for your banana split at the ice cream shop and finally hear your name called? Your servers' voices ring with excitement, while they watch to see your expression as you feast your eyes on the superb masterpiece of divine dessert they hand crafted for you. Well this moment wasn't like that. It was more like, "I've been here 82 hours today, I haven't seen the sun, I had Jell-O for lunch, I'm underpaid, I'm overweight from sitting in my adjustable swivel chair 10 days a week, and I'm not a people person; now sit here while I jab you with this needle." I had immediate suspicions as to why the girls were white as ghosts when they left the clinic! My ears cringed at the sound of my name as I looked up and saw the person calling me to the *other* side of the office.

Oh, how I didn't want to go. That was the longest four-second walk of my life! But there I stood, on the other side, the side where life-changing decisions were made.

Part 1, Chapter 11
A Life-Changing Decision

The appointment was made, and the day came quickly. This is where a lot of details get blurry for me. I don't remember much before the IV. I guess the details were small enough that I've just forgotten. But the IV and the doctor, I will never forget! First of all Helga, the blind nurse with a nerve disorder, administered my IV. Her hair was in a bun, and she had bumpy lips. I remember her lips so well because I couldn't understand a word she said, which left me watching her mouth when she spoke. I may have been the very first person she ever poked with a needle.

Just before I met the anesthesiologist who would, thankfully, put me to sleep for the procedure, I met the doctor for the first time. I don't recall his name, but I remember his face and his voice. He had deep-blue eyes, and his skin was pitted. He was very pale, possibly dead. His voice was dull and dreary, monotone, in fact. He appeared bored. I was just another number in his appointment book. However, he did hold my hand while explaining to me what would take place while I was sleeping. The doctor informed me he would be using the vacuum procedure. Before that week, I had never heard of it. He went on to describe how he would dilate my cervix, and then vacuum the "fetus" out. He said I would experience some cramping for the first few days and to expect some mild to moderate bleeding for a couple weeks afterwards. Then I would be back to "normal." "Any questions," he asked.

"No." I thought to myself, "I can't believe I'm doing this." I didn't even have the chance to grasp or comprehend what the doctor just explained to me. Before I knew it, a man in white was counting me off to sleep. The last words I heard were, "Soon it will be all over." The next words I heard were, "It's all over!" Well that's great I suppose. I have had several surgeries since where I've been put under anesthesia. Each time I've awakened without commotion. At times, I've been cold and shaky but mostly happy, but not on this day.

Before the surgery, I was full of fear; quiet, and cooperative. But I woke up a different person. I was full of anger. It was anger beyond my control. An anger so raging that I actually slapped the nurse's face that arrived with the puke bucket just in time. I remember looking around and seeing several other girls just waking up or recovering. I was so enraged at them for being there. I didn't want anyone to see me. I just wanted to be alone and go home. The nurses wouldn't leave me alone. They insisted on helping me. I didn't want to be helped. The more they tried, the angrier I became. I'm sure no one was in danger, but I could still yell, and I tried that too! They moved me to another area, a very small, stark, cold white room. A nurse sat in a chair, safe in the corner, to monitor me but left me completely alone. And that's where I would wait for the next couple hours, alone and crying, exactly what I needed. The pain was unbelievable. It was like nothing I had ever felt before. If they had left me for dead, I'd have been entirely fine with that.

I had no idea how drastically the course of my life just changed. All things that were to come and all decisions I was yet to make would be affected as a result of that one afternoon. I didn't realize from that day forward my life would never be the same. A 16-year-old girl changed forever. Eventually, enough time had passed that the nurses felt it was safe (for others probably) to release me.

They helped me get dressed while explaining all the post surgery care instructions, none of which I wanted to hear or remember. When I was ready, they led me to a small room where only my boyfriend sat, waiting. This was the room with the "secret exit." Instantly, it occurred to me why I never saw some of those girls come back out through the waiting room. They didn't allow the ones who just had an abortion to leave through the main lobby. If I had seen a girl walk out after her abortion a week ago, I may not have followed through. I'm sure a private exit was to protect the patient's privacy. Can you imagine how that might have shaken up some of the girls to watch someone walk past in a state similar to what I was in at that moment? I wonder how many would have changed their minds. Would I have? But there I was leaving with a prescription for pain meds and a pack of birth control pills.

The ride home was quiet. The longest 30 minutes ever. I cried softly to myself while trying to hide the excruciating pain. We didn't say much. I guess not a lot could be said. It was over. Everything had been taken care of. Still, I was growing more concerned at how I would cover this all up. I clearly wasn't looking very good. What would I tell my friends? When we arrived home, our friend who let us borrow the money for the procedure was waiting for us. There was an awkward silence as we just stood there. The guys certainly didn't know what to say. Congratulations? When I couldn't stand it any longer, I blurted out, "Let's go celebrate!" Next thing I knew, the three of us were sitting in a restaurant laughing and going on like nothing ever happened. I sat there and pretended all night that I was so excited. I explained to them everything I could remember. I even bragged about how angry I was when I slapped the nurse. I hid the physical pain and shoved down what was truly going on inside. I put on a brave face and made light of it all. They seemed to be impressed. After that day, we never talked about it again.

Before I knew it, I was back to "normal" just like the doctor said. No one suspected a thing. Maybe that "flu" I suffered had finally run its course. So it was life as usual spending long days at the beach, working at fast-food restaurants in the evenings and going to parties late at night. What a life I surround myself with. Well, I was miserable. Looking back now, I recognize that, but I sure was fooling myself then. How do I know this? I was on a desperate mission for fulfillment. My long days on the beach were all about getting noticed. Looking good in my bikini and making sure people saw that. I actually hated the night parties. I hated feeling that I had to claim my boyfriend so that no other girl would take him. So I would do whatever he wanted to make him happy and to stay near him.

That usually meant drinking and smoking, not cigarettes either. Some nights I would have to be carried to the car and would hear my "friends" laughing yet thinking to myself, "Good, I'm making them happy." The next morning would be an instant reminder of humiliation - if I remembered a thing at all. So another day would begin again. I would make my way to the beach and occasionally get some bad vibes from my girlfriends; that usually meant either their boyfriend or I had been too friendly the night before. So I would spend a bigger part of that day trying to get blanks filled in and friendships repaired only to repeat the cycle in a matter of hours. Yes, I was full of joy (or so I thought)! I was exhausted. Worn out from trying to maintain a life that I felt I couldn't change. If I can't change it, then I would have to make it work. That was logical to me.

Never mind that I was empty, unhappy, afraid, and lost. I sank into an acceptance that this is where I must settle. This is my life, the hand I was dealt; therefore, I must play it.

Isn't it interesting how I worked so hard at hiding everything? Why would I do that? No one ever told me the way I lived my life was wrong. Nobody ever suggested abortion was wrong. And I certainly had no spiritual influence on my life telling me the choices I was making were wrong, yet I hid the abortion anyway. On the outside, it's interesting that I appeared stoic and arrogant; but on the inside, I was full of shame and disgrace. I was scared. But what would compel me to feel that way?

Part 1, Chapter 12

The Second Offense

It's hard to believe I'm writing a chapter about a second abortion. I have to inject here, that today, I feel so detached from that person. It's as if while writing this and recalling these memories, I'm looking at some other woman, not me. Not the person I am now. But, that was me in September of 1988, just barely over one year after my first abortion, suspecting I might be pregnant again.

I was nearing 18 years old and going nowhere rapidly. My boyfriend and I were still together and had our own apartment. We felt legitimate, but the relationship was bitter. I couldn't begin to tell you what it was based upon. We were together for convenience; I suppose. I'm not really sure. We both knew for certain we would not be together forever. And there you have it, another reason to justify my next abortion. It was one more excuse to help me rationalize my behavior.

That same September, my grandmother lay in the hospital with cancer. I loved my "Baba" very much. I have many wonderful memories with her. Some of my favorites involve food. She was a crazy eater! And I must confess I have passed some of Baba's food fun on to my own children. Like warm flour tortillas spread with butter and sprinkled with sugar, rolled up and eaten like a burrito. Or fresh bread dipped in dark Karo syrup. Baba loved her sweets! And I loved going to her house!

My family and I often would visit my grandmother when she was in the hospital. However, she quickly became too ill to visit with us. I knew I wouldn't have her much longer. I wanted to tell her so badly that I was pregnant. She always felt safe to me. Nothing I had ever done disappointed her. No one else in the family knew about this pregnancy or the last one. And though I longed to say something, I just couldn't tell her, not in the state she was in. It would not have been fair. In fact, I wouldn't speak at all. I simply held her hand at her bedside recalling all our sweet memories and special times together, wishing I was a little girl again baking desserts in Baba's kitchen. That was all I wanted. I didn't want to be pregnant. I didn't want anyone to know and be disappointed. I didn't want my grandmother to leave me. But there was nothing I could do.

As I sat watching Grandma die from a disease beyond her control, I recognized the baby inside of me would soon die under my control. It's amazing how I had no regard for life whatsoever, yet I was capable of loving so deeply and sincerely. I just never could connect with the life inside of me, as if it weren't real.

The time was nearing when I would have to confirm a decision on whether or not I would have another abortion. I didn't take much time making up my mind. I was at a friend's house when I got the call from the clinic with my pregnancy test result. The appointment for the abortion was made before I hung up the phone.

I must admit it did feel somewhat awkward for me that day. The girlfriend I was visiting that afternoon was pregnant. She and her boyfriend were keeping the baby and getting married after the birth. She never tried talking me out of it either, something that I now think was rather strange. Did she not feel compelled to say something or feel anything about my situation to try to talk me out of it?

Was she afraid to? Was it her obligation or responsibility as a friend to share her feelings about my decision? Would it have mattered? We were all just so young and immature. It just proves we weren't ready for all of this. We had no business being in these situations. Babies having babies. That is very sad.

One week later that same girlfriend drove me to my appointment. It was another quiet long trip, which added to the awkwardness. I can't imagine how much more uncomfortable she was. It wasn't even the silence that was unnerving. It was what we weren't saying. She and I talked about everything under the sun: ex-boyfriends, gossip, fashion, music, but not one thing about what was just about to happen. What would we have said to each other? Should I have told her that she was making a mistake by keeping that child inside of her? Should she have told me that I was making a mistake by killing the child inside of me? "Yes." "No." It was not her fault that she didn't say anything, and that I went through with the procedure anyway.

As a friend, I believe there is an obligation to say something. If you are a friend of someone who is considering an abortion, I believe wholeheartedly it is your obligation to start a dialogue with her. Do not delay.

I looked over at her several times during the trip as she silently drove. I knew she wanted to say something to me. It was clear just by her body language alone. She seemed tense and disappointed. She was far enough into her pregnancy that she was beginning to show a little bit. She radiated with beauty too. She was such a contrast with me in the other seat. Abortion number two, no plans on getting married, no plans at all. Just living for the moment and dealing with the consequences later.

The second abortion was harder. The procedure itself was much more painful than the first one. It was different from the first one. It was the same clinic but a different doctor and nurses. Because I was already on file, there were fewer steps to take before the actual surgery. They already had all my information. Admittedly, it was a little embarrassing during check-in when they said, "Oh, this is your second termination. You already know what to do." Lovely...Repeat Offender! Even though the decision to have this abortion was easier, it did affect me more emotionally. I suspect that had a lot to do with my Baba being so close to death.

My heart seemed tender. I was considering how horrible of an act I was committing. I did think about the baby, and it really occurred to me that this was number two! When would it stop? If I got pregnant a third time, would I choose to have another abortion? Would I really want to do that again? I was even more lost and confused a year and a half later. No personal growth, no lessons learned.

Part 1, Chapter 13
The Escape

Who is this person staring back at me? My reflection looked nothing like I had always imagined. At least I didn't feel like the princess I dreamed of becoming when I was a little girl. Instead, the young woman staring back at me looked lost and afraid. With silent tears streaming down my face, I stared blankly out the Greyhound Bus window. I shook my head in bewilderment as I recounted the last five days of my life.

How did I get here? Why am I on this bus?

I was terrified of buses as a child. And I certainly didn't care much for them now. I remembered my mother having to force me onto the school bus when I was in kindergarten. Each school morning would begin with tears, knowing I soon would have to face the big yellow trap of doom, which quickly escalated into a full-blown anxiety attack, complete with the runs. Yes, this was every morning, without fail.

The walk to the bus stop was treacherous. My little 5-year-old legs would move extra slow as my mother kept firmly tugging my arm, hurrying me to the corner pick up. We would stop about four houses away, and she would push me on alone to the corner. Cutting my normal stride in half, I'd eventually make it to the bus stop where I would stand crying as loud as I possibly could. Secretly, I was hoping a *caring* mother would stop, scoop me up, and never make me ride that scary bus again, but it never happened. My own mother stood a half a block away, watching me carrying on like a blind cat thrown into the center of the ocean...whatever that looks like. I can imagine it would look pretty pathetic.

After some time, the bus would come. I can still hear the screeching, high pitched squeal of the brakes. I can smell the brakes. I can almost taste the exhaust. Oh, and the sound of the bus doors opening...I think I'm having a mini panic attack just recalling this scene. Gradually, my little buster brown shoes would hit the first step of the bus. I'd look up at the driver who glared back at me. I imagined her saying, "If your mama wasn't standing right down the street, I'd yank your little crying hiney straight onto this bus!" Fortunately for me, she never had to resort to that.

Finally, I would make my way down the center aisle, looking for an empty seat among a land of giants, carrying on with my tears and snot bubbles. I'd squirm my way into a small space, sit there, afraid...and continue to cry.

Fourteen years later, I found myself, again, on a bus...afraid...in tears. But this time was different. I wasn't reluctant to go. As uncomfortable as I was sitting in the bus, all I wanted was for it to take me away. In fact, it couldn't drive off fast enough!

Taking quick, slightly frantic breaths, I realize I have just escaped with my life! The man I just said, "I DO" to five days earlier, has just become public enemy #1.

"Why isn't this bus going?"

I close my eyes and try to calm my thoughts, my breath. My hands won't stop shaking. My feet won't stop jittering. The person next to me is clearly agitated. I cannot ease my mind.

My first flashback hits me like a pain from a knife wound to the chest. I'm on the floor, next to his side of the bed as he straddles over me – yelling – swinging his fists – making contact with my flesh. I beg him to stop. He tells me I deserve this. I close my mouth and surrender. I stop trying to protect myself. I pull my hands away from my face and give up. I give my husband what he wants. I take a couple more hits. They burn. They sting. They're loud. They satisfied his rage. At least, temporarily...

"Excuse me, ma'am...Are you okay? Ma'am?" A man's hand grabs my right arm. I quickly swing it back in defense. We lock eyes, and my thoughts wander back...

Life was really good. Having left my beloved West Coast only 10 months prior in hopes of starting over and bettering my life, I was ecstatic to have landed a job at a popular little furniture store in Knoxville, Tennessee. I ended up in Knoxville after my brother had asked if I would come stay with him and his family there for a while. I was in desperate need of a change, so, I decided to take him up on his offer. Never, ever, imagining I'd live anywhere else besides the beautiful West Coast, I found myself enjoying the beauty of the East. The accents were a little much, but the people were pleasant. I worked in the finance and inventory office doing a little bit of everything, including catching the eye of my boss's best friend who was also one of the most beloved people in Knoxville.

Before long, like one week before long, I was slow dancing to country music with this city's beloved man in a bar - with a drink in hand - illegally. I was just a baby at 19. Beloved was 15 years my senior at the age of 34. He was my safe father figure who had come to my rescue. Finally, everything was going to be perfect.

"Ma'am? Are you okay?" It's the gentleman sitting next to me on the bus. He noticed that I was clearly shaken, dreading sitting next to him. Then, I realized he only wanted to know that I was alright. I take a deep breath and tell him I'm fine. Thinking to myself, "What do you care? You're a man. I am nothing to you."

I begin looking around the bus as people slowly board. I'm frightened that he might find me; that he might discover I've escaped. Increasingly growing more fidgety and nervous I, once again, close my eyes in an attempt to block everything out for a moment. However, the occurrences of recent days are too fresh, just too frightening for me to shake off. For a brief second, I secretly wished he had pulled that trigger.

Less than 24 hours before, a gun's barrel was digging into my chest. With my back pressed up against our front door, his gun pointed at my heart, his eyes screamed to me that all he wanted was to make me as miserable as he was...even to death. And to think, just a few days prior to this we were both sharing our vows together before his entire family and a handful of friends. Even then I knew this was a mistake. Just seconds before I said, "I do," something in my gut was telling me to run.

The bus window rattles. Tap. Tap. Tap. I keep my head forward and refuse to open my eyes. I know it's him. He found me. This is it. This is the end. My eyes are squeezed so tightly that my tears have no room to escape. How did he find me? Maybe the man next to me will help; I think.

"Tammy! Tammy! Get off the bus!"

I have gone through many traumatic moments in my life, but never once, until this very second, had I ever felt my heart genuinely hurt with pain. Struggling to breathe, I slowly turned toward the window. It's my brother. My brother - the one who just two days before told me I ended up just like our mother and refused to help me. My brother. He's here.

"Tammy! Get off the bus!"

I yell back through the window that I am not leaving the bus. I can't go back. I won't go back.

"Just come to the door, Tammy."

"Ma'am? I'll save your seat." The tears find their way out. I agree…I meet my brother at the front of the bus.

"He was here, Tam."

"What do you mean he was here? Why are YOU here?"

"I heard that you got a bus ticket and left. I thought I'd follow you, just in case. He followed you, too. I ran him down. I told him, 'If you dare get on that bus to get my sister, I will kill you.' He left."

For the second time in our lives, we hugged. I fell into my brother's arms, and wept, and he held me. He told me he would wait until the bus left, and he knew I was safe.

Last call to board the bus came over the station's loudspeaker. My brother walked me back to my seat where the stranger waited to hold my spot.

"I'll be standing right outside this window. I won't leave till I can't see you anymore. You'll be okay."

And with that, my brother walked off. The bus backed out of the station as he stood there, keeping guard.

"Ma'am? I don't know where your final destination is, but I will stay with you as long as I can."

I don't know where my final destination will be either.

Part 2
Choosing Freedom

There comes a time in your life when you know that what you have been through has shaped you, but you choose to not let it control you.

There is so much power in our ability to choose. How we respond is solely up to us.

Part 2, Chapter 1
Every End Is A New Beginning

June 11th, I arrived in Southern California, met by my Uncle who was anxiously waiting to scoop me up. Uncle Rick always told me I was his favorite niece. He even shouted it once at a family reunion! Yah, that was a scary moment with all the cousins. He told me the car ride to his home would be long and was concerned that I would be uncomfortable. It couldn't be any longer than the excruciating three-day bus ride I had just been on. Within the first mile, safely in my Uncle's backseat, I fell deeply asleep - my first real rest in nearly a week.

When we walked into his home, the phone was ringing. Uncle Rick rushed to answer it. He spoke for a moment repeating, "Oh-no" several times before handing me the phone as I am just barely walking into the house.

"Hello?" I listen. I freeze. I couldn't believe her words. I didn't believe her words! My mother told me my husband had shot himself.

Silence.

It didn't even occur to me he might be dead. There was no way he would kill himself...he'd rather haunt me. After all I experienced with him in Knoxville, TN, all the abuse, all the guilt treatments, there was no way he would let me escape that easily. So I asked if he was really gone and she said, "Yes."

My legs gave out, and I hit the floor, crying, and afraid that he wasn't dead...scared that he wanted me to believe he was dead while he came after me. I was afraid my husband actually WASN'T dead. Wow! How quickly I had become a broken little girl.

"Are you sure? Are you sure?"

That's all I could say to my mother on the phone. She continued to reassure me the news she received was accurate and direct from a mutual friend who lived right above us in the apartment complex. He was found dead, on his bed, from a fatal gunshot wound to his heart. He had killed himself the day I left. Even so, in my mind, I believed he was crazy enough to fake his death and have me believe I was "safe," only to come find me when I least expected it, when my guard was down.

I was paranoid. I was exhausted. I was lost. I was so afraid. I knew his death was my fault. I was convinced he killed himself just to get at me, to make me feel bad for leaving. One last act of control.

It took several long days for me to relax. There wasn't a moment when I was not looking over my shoulder. I expected my husband to appear at any moment - figuring he would just jump out of a bush as I walked by and the horror would begin again. I would be his victim, and that would be my fate. That is what I was still preparing for. Wow, it took so long before I began thinking clearly again.

One morning, after a restless night's sleep, I woke in a fit of panic. I realized...I'm on my own! This is it. This is my life, and I have to start living it. I went from a little girl, to a married young lady, to a widow, straight to a young woman all alone with nothing. I realized I needed a job. I have to take care of myself now. There was no one else to do so. I decided I needed to suck it up, be a big girl, and move on. Honestly, I had no other choice. There were no other options. I had to stand up tall. I had to stand up for me.

I hit the pavement. I took the city bus everywhere

and handed in job applications to places that were hiring and even places that weren't hiring. Nothing was off limits. Within three days, I was employed as a Purchasing Agent for a small company in Southern California. I wasn't skilled for the job, but somehow I got it.

My first full workday hadn't even ended when a gentleman there reached out to me. Seriously. That was the last thing I wanted. I wanted nothing to do with the opposite sex. Don't look at me. Don't talk to me. Don't breathe in my general direction. Nothing. Please. Just leave me alone. But he wouldn't. He was relentless. He was also completely different than anyone I had ever met. There was something about him that was gentle and sincere. He befriended me. Although reluctant at first, I accepted his friendship in the workplace with an unspoken caution. I second-guessed every word he said.

About two weeks later, my new friend invited me to church. Church? Are you serious? *Me? In a church?* Afraid the building might spontaneously combust upon my entrance, I agreed to go anyway. If nothing else, it would be entertaining. And I certainly needed some comic relief in my life.

He and his family picked me up early that next Sunday morning. I sat in their backseat a nervous wreck sweating, shaking, and nauseous. I couldn't believe I was going to church. The last time I had been in a church, I was 11 years old. I used to go with my grandparents to their church on the second Sunday of every month. Why the second Sunday, you ask? Because that was the Sunday they served cookies and hot chocolate before services. I was an opportunist. I knew a good moment when it was offered.

My new friend, his family, and I walked through the church doors. I don't work out, so I am unaccustomed to sweat, but in this moment...I was sweating oceans. Immediately, people came up to my workplace friend. He introduced me to them all as, "The one you've been praying for."

Huh? What does THAT mean? Who are these people and why are they praying for me? I don't need prayer. And they were all really nice. For me, uncomfortably nice; but, I smiled and played along with the niceties.

My new friend invited me back to church week after week. And, strangely, I was compelled to go. However, each and every time I became increasingly intrigued by everyone's happiness. I wanted what they had. I needed what they had.

Sunday, August 19th, 1990 there was a guest speaker at church. His name was Mardo. Mardo had a very strong accent of some kind, not sure what it was. In fact, I could not understand one thing he said. I sat there in the back row, listening intently, trying to read his lips to follow along. I wanted so badly to know what he was talking about. After about 40 minutes, as he was drawing to a close, it all became clear. I heard Pastor Mardo for the first time. I heard actual words. In one closing sentence, I understood him. This is what he said:

"Ipp inee ub you wood like to uh-sept Sheesis Klighst indoo yaw hourt, pluhze pay wit me..."

(Translation: "If any of you would like to accept Jesus Christ into your heart, please pray with me...")

As strange as those words sounded to my ears, their meaning caught the attention of my shattered and frightened heart. As I bowed my head, my thoughts went back to my childhood - all the fear, the physical abuse, the secret abuse. My thoughts drifted to the teenage girl in the abortion clinic where I was on two separate occasions. Then my thoughts settled on my most recent journey...my husband holding a gun to my chest, and me sneaking off to the Greyhound Bus Station, barely escaping Knoxville, TN. I shuddered as I pondered my three-day trip to California. I relived being told that my husband committed suicide.

Then, all those thoughts and images disappeared. All

I could see now was God. Not in a physical sense, but it was...Him. Everything else disappeared. All the fear and confusion - gone. In that single moment there was nothing but breath. And I heard the words, "I brought you here." I knew right then, without question, God had been with me all along. He brought me here...back to Southern California - to my new job, my new friend, and to this church. Everything, for the first time in my life, made sense.

The next thing I heard was, "Amen."

I left the building a brand new person that Sunday. Everything in me changed in an instant. I was determined to live. I wanted to live. For the first time, I was looking forward to life. I realized in a powerful way, my life had just been radically changed in every sense of the word...my life had been saved.

And, on that same day, I had no idea the love of my life was also sitting in that building. But God did. He knew all along.

Part 2, Chapter 2
The Missing Link

Today, he describes me as the "L.A. Gear chick" the first time he saw me walk into the church. Thankfully the building didn't spontaneously combust upon my entrance. Granted, it was 1990, but I was still hanging onto 1989. I strutted my stuff into the sanctuary wearing a jean mini-skirt, a cropped-top with a cropped acid-washed jean jacket, white scrunchy socks, and white and blue high-top L.A. Gear sneakers. Oh-Yes-I-Did!

It was barely one month after fleeing Knoxville, narrowly escaping with my life from my, now dead, abusive husband. Unbeknownst to me, I had managed to catch the eye of a dashing, young, tanned, Southern California boy. Sure, I noticed him too when I walked in. I thought he was cute. Being a church boy and all, I also thought he'd be odd.

It was a Thursday night and my friend from work, who had brought me along to church with him, also invited me to "Worship Team Practice." That was the strangest thing I had ever heard. And I've heard some strange things in my life. My first thought was, "You have to practice worship? Are you not allowed to worship until you pass a test? Will there be a grading panel? I want to grade!" It was all so foreign to me.

I take a seat in the mostly empty room, and I try not

to reveal too much leg sitting there in my jean mini-skirt. I spot some folded half sheets of paper on the floor around me and use those to put across the tops of my legs pretending to read them as if I were interested. On one sheet I remember something about an "Elder Meeting" and an "All Church Buffet." On another, there were lots of words like, "Hosanna, Praise, Kingdom, and Doxology." I always thought doxology was a breed of dog. I was so confused. Then, out of the corner of my eye, I see the tanned boy walk onto the stage and take his place behind the keyboard. What? Tanned and a musician? Oh dear. Please let him have a doxology, too! He'd be the perfect guy. Wait. AND a microphone? Who IS this boy?

After several weeks of sitting in on these Worship Practices and Sunday services, I began to get more comfortable in their surroundings. People were befriending me and I, truly, started liking them. Trusting them. Wanting to know more about them. As mentioned in the previous chapter, I "Uh-septed Sheesis," and my life immediately experienced change. Instead of going to church with my friend out of obligation, I felt compelled to go. I wanted to be there more than anything.

One beautiful sunny Sunday afternoon, after all the church festivities were over, a bunch of us headed to lunch. My friend drove me to the restaurant and mentioned the tanned boy, who had left for the restaurant before us.

"You know, Tam; he likes you!"

"He does?" My bladder instantly fills up because, for some reason, this is what happens to me when I get nervous.

"Yes, he does. I've known for a few weeks. He was talking about you to me as he shared his interest in you. But also, he said he was not going to date someone who didn't believe in God. He knew it wouldn't make sense, and he didn't want to fall for someone who hasn't fallen for Jesus."

"Um. Okay."

"Great part about this, Tam, is that I never told you

any of it until now. I purposely kept it from you. You came to God on your own, in your own time. It was just about you and the Lord...no one else."

We pull into the parking lot and I, very unladylike, run into the restaurant, fly past tanned boy, and head straight for the bathroom. On one hand, I am relieved and on the other, I am filled with panic. It's only been two months since my marriage ended in suicide, I thought to myself. This can't be right.

Next thing I know, I'm wearing out my first, ever, Christian music cassette tape and driving around town with tanned boy in his lowered, red, Nissan pick-up truck. I know. You read that right...a lowered truck. He also wore fluorescent yellow volleyball shorts, but at least he played volleyball. Have I mentioned the beginnings of his treacherous mullet that was slowly taking up space down the back of his tanned neck? Still, something in me knew he was safe and that this was okay...despite his vehicle and fashion choices.

And just like that, we're spending every free moment with each other. Dating, I guess. All I remember now is that six weeks into our "relationship" I asked him when he was going to ask me to marry him. Look...I had already experienced quite the life; there was no time to mess around with warm fuzzies and mysteries. I had to know if I needed to fully un-guard my heart with him and how long that was going to take. His answer to my offbeat question about a marriage proposal, "Well, I guess, now?" That night, October 10th, 1990, we were engaged.

Okay, let's do the math here. On June 11th, I arrived in Southern California after a long three-day Greyhound escape bus ride. At the beginning of July, I accept an invitation to church from a co-worker. The next month, Aug 19th to be exact, I recognize my need for God, and just days after that the boy and I start dating. Six weeks later, I'm engaged. That's four months from the time my first husband held a shotgun to my chest, ultimately taking his own life. Now I am across the country, a whole new person and engaged to be married to a boy I've known for barely three of those months. I think this qualifies as crazy, don't you?

How could I jump in so quickly? Was I out of my mind?

It's probably safe to say that, yes, I might've been slightly out of my mind. But in a good way, if that makes sense. For the first time, I wasn't thinking with the same mind I had always thought with. I was changing, even if it had been only four months and the start of my transformation journey. I was different. I walked differently. I stood taller. I took deeper breaths. I actually remember taking deep breaths, the kinds of breaths people take when they're comfortable in their surroundings. All my life I spent on guard, standing post for my own safety, with bated breath.

I love hearing my tanned boy husband, Brent, tell the story of how he saw me change right before his eyes in the days following my decision to believe in God.

> *"You've heard of stories where people have instant transformation, instantly putting into the ground the old self and raising up a new creation! That was Tam. That's exactly what happened. It was her time."*
> *(Brent's comments)*

He's right. That's how it happened. And because I gave in, gave up, and gave over my fight, God had a completely clean and willing slate to work with. Would there still be struggles to come? You betcha. Lots of them! But in those first moments of revelation, it was go time...time to start anew. That is exactly why I felt the freedom and security to date Brent. I saw him with different eyes. I didn't look at him through the lens of horror that had recently been framed around my eyes. Those old spectacles were removed. I didn't label him an abuser, quitter, or offender based on the models that had been lived out before me. My perspective on life and hope in people had changed so dramatically. Mainly because of the new environment I found myself in, and partly because Brent had something no one else in my life ever had...God. The missing link. The beginning of my second chance.

Part 2, Chapter 3
A Mini-Truck Revelation

It was a beautiful day in sunny Southern California. Brent and I were newly dating, newly in gaga over each other, and newly smitten with every single word the other one spoke. We loved being together, and we snatched up every opportunity we could to make it happen, even if it meant just driving around the city with the windows down. Although, I was not a fan of Brent's vehicle. It was that lowered mini-truck. SO very much lowered that he had to slow down for cigarette butts in the road so as not to destroy its frame or something.

Brent's truck had other custom features. My favorite? Monogrammed headrests. Right? I know, pretty killer for a 19-year-old. On one headrest, there was a beautiful embroidered B on it, for Brent. The other? A beautiful S, for his ex-girlfriend...Give it a moment. It'll hit you. Moving on. This particular afternoon with Brent has stuck in my mind for over 20 years now. Because we were a new couple, we still had a lot to learn about each other. For example, why does he have a mini-truck? It boggled my mind. Brent knew that I had been in a marriage that ended in suicide, but I only shared with him a small portion of my past. I didn't want to scare off this adorable boy and his mini-truck. Wait, that's a half-truth. But the parts he knew deeply affected him for they were completely different from anything he had ever experienced or heard before. He would ask questions that always caught me off guard, but he didn't want to know the gory details of my story. He wanted to know what I was thinking during those times. Brent was concerned with how those past moments made me feel. It was almost as if he wanted to try on my story for himself, perhaps to feel what I felt. I found it a bit odd. So that, coupled with his mini-truck, was growing into a mild concern for me.

Then he said something that made it all clear in an instant. "Tammy, I wish I had a testimony."

Listen…I was new at this Christian stuff. The only time I ever heard the word testimony up to this point was when one of my friends had a court date. Working hard to switch my thinking gears, I sat quietly for a bit when finally, it occurred to me, and so I asked, "Brent, is not having a testimony actually a testimony?"

He continued looking straight ahead as he drove around the city. "I don't know. What do you mean?" He asked.

"Well, I would think that not doing some of the things I have done would be much harder than just giving in and doing them. I guess the way I see it is that not having a testimony, at least like mine, would require a lot more strength and smarts."

Trisha Davis, one of my good friends, and I were recently having coffee and chatting about her and her husband's ministry and book. Trisha and her husband Justin travel and speak on the topic of marriage. They had gone through a very traumatic jolt in their relationship when it was discovered that Justin was having an affair. Their book, *Beyond Ordinary: When A Good Marriage Just Isn't Good Enough*, is about that and how God redeemed and restored their marriage. Trisha and I began discussing how it almost seems people think they need a shock value incident to have a testimony. You don't. It isn't necessary in order to have an impact.

The way I saw it that day in Brent's lowered mini-truck was completely different from how Brent viewed it. I'd rather sit in a room listening to someone like him tell me how he'd managed to dodge all the tempting apples. Cause let's be honest; those apples are being hurled at us at lightening speed in droves! So, to have the power and determination to run from them is something I want to know more about so that I, too, can dodge them. That, right there, is a testimony! I'm not suggesting that you can dodge all the apples that are thrown at you. Unfortunately, some of us are victims in our testimonies.

But, please, if you don't have a gruesome story or a tale of betrayal, do not, for one second, believe you've nothing to offer. Your story is just as important as anyone else's. Live it. Tell it. You never know whom you might encourage.

Part 2, Chapter 4
Where Did The Happy Go?

I asked my mom to attend our wedding. I wanted so badly for her to be there, but she told me she probably wouldn't make it. She and her husband and a couple others were going to Vegas that weekend. I mean, we weren't super close, obviously, regardless of how many times I reached out to her, but a mother should want to be there to see her daughter get married, right? I always wanted that super close mother/daughter relationship, but she had so much going on in her life that there seemed to be no time for that. So, as you would expect, I was pretty disappointed that she wouldn't make it to the wedding; but at least my dad and his wife were coming up from Southern CA.

It was Friday afternoon, two days before the wedding, when my dad and step-mom pulled into my driveway in Oregon. Even though I didn't have a super close relationship or history with either of them, I was still thrilled to run out to blood-family. I felt so special knowing my dad drove all the way up from Southern California to give me away at my wedding.

As mentioned already, he and I weren't very close, but he was my dad...so him being there just felt right. I ran out to greet them in the driveway. He casually stepped out of his car and gave me a side hug. Yes. A side hug. My first thought...You just could have sent me a card, dad. But, I put my best foot forward and my best smile on and tried to ensure he felt welcomed and happy.

My Gramps was also there for the wedding up from California; the one constant male figure in my whole life. Once he came into our crazy family, he claimed us all as his own. It felt so good to have him there with me, even for a short while. His presence filled my 800 square foot bungalow with much-needed light-heartedness. We talked way into the late hours each night, sharing memories of years past. The way his laughter caused his belly pooch to bounce up and down always made my heart burst!

The following day was our wedding rehearsal and rehearsal dinner. I was REALLY excited for this day to get here. Now, I wasn't that little girl who spent long days dreaming of her wedding and planning it down to the most meticulous item and detail. Honestly, there weren't a lot of weddings in my family, so it wasn't something I was actually familiar with or thought much about. You can imagine, then, that with my lack of wedding experience, I really didn't know what to expect. I think having little to no expectations benefited me greatly, and I'm not one naturally to let things ruffle me too much. If the flowers don't arrive and the bows don't match, I am not going to morph into Bridezilla. It takes a lot more than that to shake me.

Our wedding was simple, which made the rehearsal a breeze. The wedding party was small. Brent's best man was his brother, Evan. My best woman (I've always wondered why the position isn't called that) was my future mother in law, Lynda, and the Pastor was Brent's father, Kimball. The ring-bearer was Brent's cousin, Christine, who risked her life to attend. She had been in a near-fatal car accident just one-year prior, but wanted so badly to be a part of this wedding. She was the highlight of the weekend. Sadly, for us, she has since gone to be with Jesus.

And, that was it. You may have noticed that the

wedding party was very one family sided…and not mine. Yes, it was. Besides my dad agreeing to give me away, much of my side of the family had other things to do than attend my wedding.

The wedding rehearsal was over within an hour, and we all headed off to Brent's parents' house where the rehearsal dinner awaited us, poolside, in their backyard. It's the middle of August in beautiful Oregon. I couldn't wait to share the beauty of the outdoors with my dad and step-mom. At this point, I'm on cloud nine, giddy, and starving. Slowly, people start arriving. There is a lot of laughter, stories, and hugs filling the late summer, charcoal-smoked, air. While helping bring food out from the kitchen, I notice my dad sitting off in a lounge chair far back in the corner of the yard. I slow my steps and focus in a bit. He is not looking as though he is enjoying himself. In fact, he looks more like he would rather be watching clear paint dry. I look around for his wife and see her walking toward him with a folding chair in hand. She unfolds it and sits beside him. There in the corner they sat and stayed, arms crossed, surveying the ones around them.

I continue on toward my future father-in-law who is manning the grill. I hand him a platter of patties and dogs, and he takes them from my hand and says, with a huge smile on his face, "Thank you, my future daughter!"

Beyond him, in the distance, I spot my dad, again, who was not quite as jovial. He stares my way with an expressionless face. We lock eyes for a quick moment then I glance back at Brent's dad, then back again toward my dad. I step away to head inside the house for a few minutes to myself. I am deeply conflicted. I want to be happy. I should be happy. This is my wedding weekend. A wedding that, in all honesty, is a miracle to be happening at all, but I can't shake the plethora of emotions that are swirling through the backyard air. I stand inside and stare out of the large living room picture window that overlooks the entire backyard.

Within seconds, I am taken back to everything I ever knew as a child. It all feels so fresh and so very unwanted. I see all the family and friends interacting, laughing, and having fun, but there is a thickness in the air. Gazing at my dad, who still sits alone, off in the far corner of the yard, I tilt my head to the right allowing a tear to fall from my eye. Why is he so bitter? Where did his happy go? I watch a few people make their way over to him only to leave immediately after what seemed to be failed attempts at small talk. My heart is pounding so hard it hurts. I want to fix this. I want to fix him. I want to pretend the scene that I see before me is only a joke, but it isn't.

The sound of my soon to be mother-in-law's laughter quickly shakes me out of this sad reality and instantly into a new reality. My new reality. Taking a very deep breath, I fix my eyes on this family that has so lovingly welcomed me into theirs. They are laughing, chatting, and making new friends with late arriving guests. Then I see Brent's parents make their way, once again, over to my dad and his wife only to walk away within a few short minutes. I cannot get over the stark contrast of family differences. I never fully realized until that moment that my normal childhood and family life might not have been very normal. Or, perhaps these new people in my life weren't normal. I didn't know what to feel or think; but in that second I knew one thing for sure, there was a lot of hurt sitting in that far corner, and it crushed my heart. I wanted nothing more than to help him find his happy.

Why was he hurting? What did I do?

Part 2, Chapter 5
The Wrong One

He was my father. That is why I asked him to give me away at my wedding. I have always been afraid of hurting people's feelings, so it seemed best and appropriate for me to extend this opportunity to him. For once, I actually knew where dad lived at the time. It didn't matter much to me how little history and even less connection we had, it just felt like the right thing to do. So, I had to extend the invitation for him to give me away. However, I realized within minutes of his arrival that giving him this privilege had been a big mistake. I will not go into details or statements made, but I will share that just barely seconds before he walked me down the aisle, just before the ushers opened the doors into the sanctuary where my "happily ever after" awaited my arrival, dad said the most hurtful thing to me.

"Tam...you and your new family have really disappointed me."

My heart stopped, all joy was erased from my face, the excitement and thrill that had resided in every vein during my groom's and my engagement...gone. Tears filled my eyes; I slowly lifted my head, turned to my dad, and said, "I'm sorry."

Inside I was screaming, "Really? We have disappointed you, Dad? How so? By welcoming you into the family? By Brent's parents taking me in as their own daughter? By hosting you and your wife and treating you like royalty to ensure your comfort during your visit? How have we disappointed you? Was it the fact that we embraced you even though you rejected me all those years? Perhaps it was because we didn't punish you for all the hurt you caused me? Maybe you were angry at me for wanting you, my father, to give me away at my wedding? Please tell me, Dad...I need to know."

The next thing I remember was a bright flash. Our photographer captured that very moment as the ushers swung open the sanctuary doors. It's a photo I still would rather not look at in our wedding album. It holds so many unwanted memories. When I have chosen to look at it, all I see is the three-year-old me wanting that drink of water and being met by my father who was drenched in anger at my mom. I see his lifeless face as I stared out the back of our 1971 light blue mustang while mom drove away from him never intending to look back. I see hurt. I see pain. I see regret. I see so much; yet feel so little...

The long walk to my groom quickly shifted from excitement to a soul level deep grief. I can't even see Brent waiting for me through the size of my pain-filled tears. As dad and I walked closer toward the stage at the front of the sanctuary, I spot my precious Gramps standing in the front row – his short little self with his pudgy belly and his eyes filled with tears. While fighting back the salty pain dripping down my face, memory after memory began rushing through my mind of my Gramps and me. How he married into our family when I was just three years old, right around the time my father left. Gramps owned his role as instant grandpa. He stepped in when others stepped out. He helped pull out my first tooth with a string tied to it and a door handle that he slammed shut. Bye-bye, tooth. Gramps gave me my first bowl haircut. He literally put a big bowl on top my head and cut the loose hairs around it. He stole me for summers and let me be his secretary at his CPA's office. He experienced life with me. He chose to experience life with me. He gave me good memories.

The memories flipped through my mind like little colorful pages in a children's story picture book, one after another. And for a moment, I had forgotten that my heart had been crushed just seconds before. With my dad on my right, very loosely holding my arm, void of any facial expression, my Gramps and I locked eyes...his filled with tears...mine filled with regret that he wasn't the one locked onto my arm, walking me to my groom and handing me off to my "happily ever after." It is he, Gramps, who deserved that position. He was the one that never left his post.

Part 2, Chapter 6
We Are Having a Baby

When I was eleven or twelve years old, I began dreaming of what it would be like to have a family. I would imagine myself older with a couple children in a beautiful home, cooking dinner while the kiddos played by the front door waiting for their father to walk in from work. Thinking about that always made me happy. I would replay that scene over and over in my mind and dream of the day when I would care for my very own family with great joy. That's what I longed for, and deep inside I knew that's what I eventually would have.

Brent and I decided we wanted a baby. We had been married for nearly two years, and although that may have seemed too soon, we knew we were ready! The time had arrived to start our very own family. A moment just came when we were both convinced the world needed a little Hodge Clan. Once we made the decision, it was all I could think about every single second of every single day! The idea of becoming parents was beyond exciting to me! For weeks, my focus kept turning to pastels and maternity clothes. Each time we watched a movie I would sit through to the very end to read the entire list of credits hoping a unique name would jump out at me. I was consumed.

And I did the math. I computed the numbers several

times every day. If we have a baby now, I will only be 40 when she graduates. Then maybe 45 when I become a grandma. Ooo! Then I'd be that cool young grandma. Mmm, we should get started.

So we did. We got started. Alright, isn't that the most awkward thing? People telling you they're trying to have a baby. That's like saying, "We have sex as much as possible. Will you pass the salt, please?"

We got pregnant right away. In fact, I remember when and where. It was August 1993, at a youth event in Washington. No, we were not the youths. Been there, done that, no thanks, but we were the guests for the weekend. Brent was asked to come up and lead worship for a church's high school camp, and we had private quarters. Ta-Da! Of course, I didn't know the outcome until about one month later when I was visiting my mom in Missouri.

While in Missouri, I began to suspect I might be pregnant. There were no signs. I suppose I just had a gut feeling. I've actually heard of women who have so desperately wanted to be pregnant that their bodies will experience pregnancy symptoms even though they are not. That easily could've been me. I didn't mention to my mother that I had suspicions. One evening while she, my two sisters, and I watched a movie, I snuck into the bathroom during a commercial break and took a pregnancy test. Okay, I brought one with me just in case!

Scene: A 12 x 60 single-wide trailer, the temporary home for my family while they built my mom's dream house on the same property. I'm in the one and only bathroom straddling over a plywood-covered hole in the floor in front of the toilet attempting to pee on a stick. This was no easy task, people. I am certain the sight was beyond comical! The plywood cover was just barely too small to cover the entire hole, so if your feet hit it wrong it would wobble terribly and threaten you with a two-foot death fall to the earth below. Like a pro, I managed to stay above ground, over the toilet, and successfully pee on that stick. Honestly, this is just one of the reasons why I don't like dry camping. Or camping in general. Or outhouses. Finally, the task was completed and the hands were washed. Trust me, I scrubbed them hard after that acrobatic display. And then...I waited.

T minus 5 minutes.

I stood in front of a full-length mirror in the bathroom rehearsing how I would go out and tell my mom and little sisters. I was certain I was pregnant. I just knew it.

T minus 2 minutes.

The doubt begins to creep in. The tears begin to fall. All the guilt makes an unwanted appearance that is quickly followed by fear. In my heart, I know I do not deserve to be pregnant. I don't deserve to have a child. I've already ruined my chances to have children by my very own doing. The full-length mirror no longer reflected a rehearsing, excited, and hopeful Tam. The mirror now reflected the fears that had settled deep into my heart.

DING.

My watch alarm goes off. Five minutes have passed. This is the moment. The air is laced with trepidation and excitement. I reach out my shaky hand and pull the pregnancy test off the counter. With my eyes tightly closed, I take a long deep breath, hold the stick up, and slowly peek...

+ A plus sign.

Well, that means addition. Wait...

No. That means positive. Positive. POSITIVE!

Suddenly, the mirror reflected an excited 22-year-old shoving towels under her shirt forecasting what her pregnant self might look like in months to come! I modeled my makeshift pregnant belly in every position I could and even practiced the pregnant waddle. I hold up the stick again...still positive. It wasn't a dream. Actually, it was a dream. And I could hardly believe it was coming true.

Eventually, I left the bathroom and had a celebration with my mom and sisters jumping up and down, screaming and crying happy tears. The only thing my mom said was, "It's a girl!"

Brent. I have to tell Brent, but I needed to tell him face to face. I just couldn't bear sharing with him he'd be a daddy for the first time over the phone 2,000 miles away. That didn't seem fair. And this was a surprise worth keeping. I desperately wanted to see his expression.

In the late evening after I arrived home from Missouri, I was unpacking all the things my family had sent for me to give Brent. Casually, I decided to slip in the pregnancy test without saying a word and wait to see how long it would take him to figure it out.

"Awww, here's a homemade card from my little sister for you. So sweet. Mom sent you this goofy frog pen and I have no idea why. Oh, and then there's this white stick with dried urine on it..."

His eyes got huge as he shouted, "I knew it! I knew it the day you left for Missouri. There was just something about you!"

And just like that I lost all excitement. The reality of the moment that I was pregnant again, on purpose, with my husband, and the guilt of not having told Brent yet of my abortions rushes over me. And so my struggle begins.

Part 2, Chapter 7
A Miracle is Born

Monday, April 18, 1994 at 5:52 p.m., I delivered a tiny miracle baby girl, one month early. There were no complications during the delivery. The only people in the room were my doctor, a nurse, Brent, and me. It was quiet, almost too quiet. There seemed to be a heaviness in the air, something only I was aware of. The minute she was delivered, I looked to see her in my doctor's hands, and I said, "Isn't God good?" The doctor replied, "I was just thinking the same thing."

Immediately after those words, I felt a tremendous darkness come over me; a heaviness, like a physical heaviness, on me. When I think about it, even now, I can recall very well that lost and frightened feeling. It was as though I wasn't even there. As if that wasn't even me in that bed. And that certainly wasn't my baby. I've heard all through my life that the minute you see your newborn baby you instantly bond with them. There's an immediate connection that is unlike any other in your life. I kept staring at my newborn while they cleaned her up, weighed her, and exclaimed over and over how perfect she was, but I felt nothing, at least nothing good. I wasn't feeling the waves of overwhelming love and connection. I wasn't anxious to take her home and dress her up in all her new little fashions. I didn't want to look at her. I didn't even want to hold her.

Then they brought her to me, and I thought quickly, ok…maybe I'll feel differently when she's in my arms for the first time. The nurse propped me up, gave me a brief lesson in holding a newborn baby, and then she held her out to me. I didn't reach out to take her.

The nurse patiently placed her in the cradle of my arms, but I could barely look at her. I don't know if I resented this baby for being chosen, or if I resented me. Certainly with her early birth, we ran the risk of complications, and God could snatch her away from us. Surely, I would deserve that. I expected it. I clearly had no concept of God's love and forgiveness, but through it all, I never let anyone know of my struggle.

It wasn't long before I had sunk into a deep depression. Within hours of the delivery, actually, but I managed to hide it. Oh, how the nighttime hours were the worst. Anyone who has dealt with depression knows how dreadful the "dark" hours are. After three weeks, I couldn't bear it any longer and I had a "coming out" party. That's sort of my pattern. I get to the end of my rope and just give up…mostly. I had just gotten out of the shower when another wave of fear and despair flooded my entire being. I thought of my newborn little girl down the hall, sleeping in her crib. I imagined her not being there anymore. I imagined that her not being there might be from my own hands. I walked out of my bathroom into my room and fell to the floor next to my bed and screamed. I cried. I cried hard. I cried so hard I couldn't breathe. I begged God to save my little girl because I wanted to make everything disappear in that moment. I wanted to end the pain.

Knock-Knock.

Are you kidding me? Now?

I throw on my robe and run to my front door. I look through the peep hole and see it is my good friend. I opened the door and fall into her arms. Her words…

"We knew it. We (her husband and her) were driving home and we both felt at the same time like we needed to come to you."

God sent them there for me. For my baby. Why do I know this? They lived 20 minutes in the opposite direction. We had lived there for seven months and they had never, once, been there to visit.

We were not on their way home. We were very much out of their way.

They stayed through the tears and didn't ask questions. They just let me cry it out. They held me until Brent got home and then quietly left.

My poor husband, what a scene to come home to: unexpected guests and a crying wife. He sat down beside me on the couch and just kept asking me what was wrong. I knew I was depressed. And I knew the "why" behind it, but I couldn't tell him the true why yet. I did admit that I was battling depression. I confessed to him the feelings I had experienced earlier of wanting to end it all for me and for our daughter. I had to tell him that I was afraid I might hurt her. I had to tell my husband that I wanted to hurt our little girl. As those words came out of my mouth, I knew why I thought I wanted to hurt my baby...it was because I had hurt two others before. I believed that God was going to take her to punish me, so I would have rather settled that myself.

Friends, you have no idea how difficult it is writing this out. Or, maybe you do. And if so, I am deeply sorry. Because the pain I know that existed in this...I wish on nobody. Ever.

Brent suggested immediately that I call his dad. I got some wise counsel from my in-laws over the phone that night. All I told them was that I was depressed. Still, no one knew about the abortions. They listened to me cry and utter indiscernible words. They prayed for me. They shared Scripture with me. They talked me down while Brent held me tight. I could not deny in that moment that God was tenderizing my heart - preparing me to come clean. Communicating this depression and my fears to others... it was a monumental moment in my life. Although I still did not tell Brent about the abortions, that night God began revealing Himself to me through my newborn daughter. As the fears and heaviness of that night began to lift from me, and as I held Kass in my arms, for the first time I really looked at her. Oh, how marvelous she was. She was so beautiful. So fearfully and wonderfully made.

My little girl, eighteen days old, lies in my arms. I let myself experience her. I focused on her shape. Her soft, new, skin. Her curly dark hair. Her little button nose. She takes a deep breath and smiles for the first time. She smiled. Brent maintains it was gas, but as I looked down at her face it wasn't her that I saw. I saw the face of Jesus. It was as if through her smile, He comforted me. And I knew then that things were about to change whether I liked it or not. The transformation had only just begun.

Part 2, Chapter 8
The Secret Revealed

It was as if a tractor-trailer carrying a load of cinder blocks had just rammed into my gut. It wasn't a physical pain. It was a deep emotional pain, at the soul's center, like my core had just been invaded and disrupted. My hands began to shake. My stomach was stirring. I felt weak. I knew something big was happening, something more on a deeper, spiritual level. My secret burden was making its way to the surface, and there was no stopping it. I was about to get rocked.

Earlier that day, I had been doing battle with the Lord, pleading my case before Him as to why I needed to protect my secret. "God, why can't I just tuck it away? Why does anyone need to know? All is fine, why disturb the peace?"

Then He responded, "Because there is no peace, Tammy." He showed me how tormented I was inside as memories, lies, and times of hiding began racing through my mind. I was preoccupied with the fear of my secret getting out. It owned me. Daily, I dredged up the past and my abortions. It weighed powerfully on me each time I gazed at my daughter. Honestly, I couldn't look at her without thinking of what I had done. My mind spent a lot of time back in that abortion clinic, set on the horrible things of my life. I allowed my hang-ups to take precedence over what should have been God's position in my life...first place in my heart and mind.

Before I knew it, my knees buckled and down I went. Everything within me gave out, and I fell to the floor. Flat out I lay, with my 5 month-old baby girl unattended somewhere else in the apartment. I cried. I ugly cried. I struggled-to-breathe cried. Pounding my fist on our tiny apartment hallway floor, I yelled out, "God, I'm done! I cannot do this anymore!"

Nothing. The air was full of nothingness. I hated nothingness. And He let me lay there. Silence. Stillness. I wanted to scream again. I wanted to take back the words I just cried out. I hated silence. Silence equated to moments of torment, as I'd allow my heart and thoughts to go back to the gutter of life that I had lived. Memory after memory made an appearance, each one pulling up a chair taunting me like schoolyard bullies.

I lay there long enough to notice my tears had slowed their pace, my lungs slowly filled with air once again, and my fists had softened their defense. And that's when I realized I had just arrived at the end of Tam's road. Now it was time to merge onto God's road. I'm not sure how much time had passed before I discovered little Kassidi lying on the floor right beside me. She must have scooted her way toward me during my holy breakdown.

I lifted my head from my hands and saw this beautiful creation, this stunning child, staring back at me. Looking into the eyes of this innocent baby girl, I immediately accepted what I must do to become the mother she ultimately needed. She needed and deserved a mother who could care for her out of love and from a depth of gratitude for the gift of life. From that moment on I no longer looked at her as a tool God may use to "get back" at me, fearing He may take her as a punishment for my abortions. I began to see her as a gift, an honor, a living example, and proof of His unconditional love.

Now that God had my full attention, and I "let" Him shake me to my core and knock some holy sense into me, I stood before a new leg of my journey. Posted at the start of this new road were signs and arrows, all pointing to one direction.

Confession.

Well, that was unfamiliar territory to me, but as Greek as it was I still knew I had to put one foot in front of the other and just begin. I had to choose. Even though each of my steps were shaky and feeble, this road's purpose became clearer. I saw freedom at the end. Freedom. So that's where the road of confession leads! I wanted; I needed desperately to arrive there. And my first stop: The home of my husband's heart.

I lay in bed for hours feeling like a deer looking straight into oncoming headlights. I went over and over in my head what God had recently been revealing to me, how I was to release my grip on the past. How I would have to let go of who I was and become who He meant me to be. This would be no easy task. I knew that letting go of my past and the guilt I carried for years would mean releasing my grasp on every piece of wreckage that was holding me down. I had convinced myself that holding on for dear life to the chaos that was tormenting my soul was far better than the risk of exposing my heart and its fragility to those who might trample all over it.

But God, being the patient gentleman He is, waited for me to stop, drop, and listen; to allow Him to speak that one sentence to me, "There is no peace." How long had He waited for me to be ready to receive those words? He could have spoken them to me years earlier, but I wouldn't have been ready or willing to hear. So in His perfect time, and in His perfect wisdom and grace, He waited for me. He desired that I understand and knew long beforehand when that perfect moment would arrive. That time indeed arrived, and

I knew what I had to do.

Telling my husband was going to be the first big girl step on this road to confession. He deserved to know. This was my life partner, the one with whom I now had a child. He needed to know…I needed him to know.

For hours, I tossed and turned over and over, just enough to wake him up. Eventually, he did wake up to ask me if I was alright. My plan worked. Can I just say here how terrified I was of confessing this truth to my husband? Every part of me was dreading this. This was the moment I had been running away from for years; but God wasn't going to let me out of this. However, that did not stop me from spending the next hour and a half trying to escape the inevitable, hoping the Lord would come back if I just put it off long enough.

Brent was so patient with me. He demonstrated three full hours of superhuman ability not to take a full bottle of sleep aid! As I sat there shaking, in fetal position, crying, and rocking back and forth, he must have been so worried, wondering what could be so agonizing for me that I just could not come out and say. In my private thoughts, I must admit, I was bargaining with God. I begged, relentlessly, for a way out while He continued to show me that He had already taken care of the way out. The vision of Jesus hanging on the cross and dying for me, and for all that I have done, gave me that final push. And with that I took a deep breath and said it…

"I had an abortion."

Silence.

Just silence. No yelling. No storming out of the room or hurling angry words and insults at me.

The emptiness in the air felt more like several days than several seconds. I slowly looked up at him as he stared back at me and asked, "That's it?"

"No, " I answered. "I had two of them. I had two abortions." He took a deep breath and nodded his head back and forth. His nods left an ache in the pit of my stomach. What was he thinking? Should I prepare to have to leave? Will I ever see him or our daughter again? I braced myself for the worst.

Then he finally said, "After all of that, Tam, I thought you were going to tell me you murdered somebody."

Sigh.

I looked up into his eyes and said, "I did."

And for the next several hours, I lie in his arms and wept as I finally shared with him the rest of my story. Brent was amazing about everything. And I told him everything, each little detail of every moment. I kept thinking...when is he going to snap? How could he sit there and listen to his bride tell him such horrible details about a person he only thought he knew? I feared he would look at me differently. Maybe he wouldn't trust me around our daughter anymore. What if I got tired of her? Would I just dump her off someplace?

Surely, I was a woman capable of doing such a thing. But that's just it! Brent was able to understand that, yes, I was a woman capable of doing those things, but I wasn't that woman any longer. Grace. That was a concept I was still trying to get used to grasping. Repairing old thought patterns had been my most difficult struggle; but it was one that now someone else whom I knew, someone I trusted, could walk through with me. Now Brent, too, was aware of my struggle, and it also allowed him to understand me better.

Things that confused him before, different habits or responses, now all made sense. He was now able to help his wife navigate through a difficult ordeal and join me on my road to recovery...a road I could not have traveled without him.

It wasn't very long after telling Brent, in fact, just the next morning, I started to feel like a brand-new person. Healing and freedom began to take up residence in me. I knew it was happening too! There was an undeniable change occurring. I felt an urgency to tell the people closest to me at that time. For me, this was equally a very important part of the process, healing through confession.

I know now it was a desire that God had placed within me so that I would experience and see freedom in telling other women my story. So I decided I would tell my best girlfriends. There were four women in my life that I looked up to and admired very much. All of them brought something unique and special to our friendship. I knew they would receive it well and not look down on me in any way. I arranged separate times to tell each of them. I felt it needed to be personal and not a group thing. Although it may have been easier to tell them all at once, I just felt I needed to do it one on one. I didn't understand why God was prompting me to share my story with my friends in this way until the day I had my third of four meetings.

I sat in my girlfriend's home preparing to tell her my shocking story while our children combat crawled, drooled all over her perfect carpet, and cooed in all different ranges and sound levels as they discovered their own voices. I got through it rather quickly while she quietly sat and stared at me. Then with the sweetest accepting and understanding smile she said, "I've always known; I just knew." How on earth does someone just know a friend has had an abortion, unless, they have had...

She then proceeded to tell me her personal story. It wasn't very different from mine. I think a majority of them happen the same way. You just don't realize how many women are carrying around their little secret. Think about it? Take my group of girlfriends; two of us five were teen statistics.

And so it began. My role in this life continued unfolding. That day God began preparing me so that I would be ready to share my story with many more people.

Part 2, Chapter 9
"Dear Diary"

Dear Diary,

I'm anxious, but not nervous. I'm scatter-brained, but clear. I'm unprepared, but ready. And now I can't get a certain song out of my head. This is the night I never thought about back in 1986 and '87 when I chose to abort two babies. But, tomorrow is the day I have been awaiting for almost five years.

What will she think? What will she say? Kassidi is such a confident young one who is very sure of who she is, and whose she is. She is unshakable at times, stoic, and in control. I often wonder what's really going on in her young mind. How many secrets does she have? Will she ever tell me? She doesn't share much with us. Kass is much like her father - works things out all on her own. I'm concerned about that honestly. I know how it feels to hold things in...to not know what to do, yet choose not to talk about it. I don't believe she is keeping anything from us that we should know about, but I fear she may someday. I pray this will be a gateway to many open discussions for the two of us.

Tomorrow, Kassidi will look at me in a whole new way. How? I do not know. But regardless, I must do this.

Part 2, Chapter 10

The Day I told My Daughter

I shared in an earlier chapter that when I had my first abortion, I wasn't thinking then that I'd be telling my own daughter now. And to be perfectly honest, I don't know; but if I had seen a vision of me confessing to my first born while my 16-year-old legs were in those stirrups, I might have changed my mind about having that first abortion. There is just no way of knowing now. Nevertheless, there we were - my precious, innocent, 13-year-old young teen, and me. She had no idea the bomb I was about to drop on her.

On this day our family was on a road trip. The boys were in one car and Kass and I were in another. And here was my plan... We'd stay in our hotel for a couple of nights. During the first evening, while the boys attend a college football game, I would share my story with Kass back at the hotel. It was the perfect opportunity and environment. No distractions, just us. No way out. Still, the closer we drew to our destination the more nervous I became about it.

"Hey Kass? You want to go to the mall before we go to our hotel?"

Knowing full well that no 13-year-old girl in the known world would willingly pass up a mall invite, it was golden. This was my ticket to avoid the perfect opportunity. Perhaps if I avoided it long enough, I'd run out of one on one time at the hotel.

"Can we, Mom?"

"You Betcha!" And off to the mall we drove.

Alright, being as I'm writing this book and I have to be truthful (not that I wouldn't be otherwise), I have to confess that at this point in the trip, aka: my delaying process, I was beginning to feel a tinge of guilt. There were people back home that knew I was planning on telling Kass that night. They invested their time in pep talks and prayer. They were going to ask me about it when we returned home. And I was slightly afraid of a few of them, so that fear, along with my new-found guilt, were the only things keeping me on the confession track... but just barely.

We walked, chatted, window-shopped, ate really bad mall food, and shopped some more until we couldn't take it any longer.

"Can we go to our hotel now, Mama?"

With beads of sweat instantly forming over my brows, I say "yes," and we head out. We get to the hotel a few miles away and start checking in. They can't find our information. We're not in the system. No Brent or Tam to be found. This is it! This is my sign. I am not supposed to tell Kass. The deal was that I would tell her THIS night in THAT hotel room. Dang...too bad...too sad.

"Oh, hold on one moment, Mrs. Hodge...I see the problem here. It was registered under another name. We have you here in the system. Your room is ready on the third floor."

"You're kidding me! I mean, you're kidding me. That's great, thank you so much!"

With key fob in hand and luggage in tow, Kass and I head up to that "perfect opportunity" on the third floor. From the hallway, to the elevator, to the hallway, to the hotel room door, Kass chats up my ear exclaiming her excitement over the new clothes she just got at the mall. I attempted to appear equally excited, and hoped I pulled it off because on the inside, I felt like dropping to the floor and faking my death. I was incredibly nervous. Like, "the first day of school in a new town, new state, with students who'd shank you if you made eye contact with them" nervous. We get to the door. The key fob works - dang. We walk into a cozy, dark room. It smelled like disinfectant, thank goodness. I flip on the light switch, and the first thing I see is a squishy, welcoming, little sofa. That's it. That's the place where our relationship will change forever.

"Mama? May I try on my new clothes and show them to you?" She asks with typical teen girl energy. Awesome, more delay. Then my heart screamed a big NO to me. I take a deep breath and say, "You know, why don't we wait on that? Come sit with me over here on the couch. I need to talk to you about something." Her excited little face becomes shades of concern. "Everything okay, Mama?" Oh, how I love when she calls me "mama."

Folks, I had been praying about this very moment for years. I prayed for the perfect words. I prayed for her heart. I prayed for perfect timing. I pleaded to God for a way out of it. But over and over again He gave me a vision of a tragic, "what if?" What if Jesus hadn't gone through with the Cross? What if He had chosen to refuse to do what God had required of Him? He could have. I am not at all suggesting that this situation bears, even one/millionth, the amount of weight that was on Jesus that day; but could my telling Kass potentially save her, or a friend of hers, from going through what I went through? Even more so, could my story possibly save a life?

Each of us takes a side of the couch. Positioning pillows and wiggling our bodies into the cushions, I take in a hefty dose of air into my lungs and slowly let it out, and with that, I begin...

Part 2, Chapter 11
Face to Face

She seems so small sitting on the other side of the couch. Her eyes are very soft and loving, her disposition sweet and gentle.

"Kass, for years I have waited to tell you this. I don't know how you're going to take this. I don't how I'm going to say it."

Her beautiful green eyes get huge. Not much scared her, but many things concerned her. She hated knowing people hurt. And in that instant, she knew I was hurting. By the look on her face, I knew she was on to me. My eyes fill up with tears, so much so I can barely see her. My heart races and my body shakes.

"Sweetie, when I was just a few years older than you, I did something terrible." A tear escapes. "I have always regretted what I've done, but never more than I do right now."

Leaning forward, she asks, "What happened, Mama? What did you do?"

As more tears fall like haunting memories down my face, I tightly squeeze the pillow close to my chest.

"When I was 16...I got pregnant."

Kass sits up a little straighter and just stares at me. She says nothing. Silence. She waits. A part of me just wanted her to guess the rest and say it for me. It would make it so much easier, but she sat in silence, staring at me, waiting.

"Mama?"

"I got pregnant, Kass."

"You did?"

"Yes, but I didn't keep it."

"What do you mean? What did you do with it? What happened to it, mama?"

I'm sure, at this moment, she thinks I'm going to tell her that I gave the baby up for adoption. She's thinking that's what "happened to it." I wanted so badly to tell her that. My heart couldn't bear telling her what actually happened to that baby. I can't bear thinking about it.

"Kass... I had an abortion."

Silence.

I look at her, just a couple feet away from me, and I want to take it all back. Everything. All my dumb choices. Me telling her I had an abortion. What's going on in her head? What did I just do? She slouches a bit and leans back into the couch. I let the regret roll down my face. Neither of us says a word. She stares at me with a blank look, and I stare back at my baby girl through tearful memories.

What have I just done? She can't handle this. She shouldn't have to handle this! I am so stupid. I drop my drenched face into my shaky hands and sob.

"Mama? I'm really sorry. Can I help you?"

Did my 13-year-old daughter just ask if she could help me? She is so strong, so stoic.

"Baby girl...There's more."

She sits back up again. "Ok?"

"Just one year after I had that abortion, I had another one."

"Why, Mama?"

I tense up, and then deeply exhale as I look into her eyes.

"I don't have a good reason, Kass, but I do have a million excuses. I can tell you this...I know it was wrong for me to have had those abortions. I didn't have to have them. No one made me. No one forced me to go through with them. I chose to do this. It was all my decision."

"Were you scared?"

"More than you possibly could ever know. In fact, that's exactly why I'm telling you this, Kass. I never, ever, want you to know what those moments were like. Let yourself learn from my mistakes, Kass. Okay?"

Part 2, Chapter 12

The Day My Mom Confessed

-As told by Kassidi

I remember the day quite well, actually. Our family was heading up North a ways to Eugene, OR. Mom and I would go shopping as my dad and brother went to the Oregon Ducks football game that evening. Surprisingly enough, I don't remember where mom and I went shopping. I know, right? A girl forgot where she went on a shopping spree. It's probably because that was the week I truly became a woman. With all the bloating and cramps, I guess my brain decided finding Midol was way more important than a super cute outfit. I do, however, remember wondering what mom was waiting so eagerly to tell me.

A few weeks prior to the trip, she mentioned she had a surprise for me. She's always been super sneaky with surprises, so I didn't really know what to expect. We arrived back at the hotel room and threw all of our bags on the bed. I plopped down on the oh-so-luxurious hide-a-bed couch. I was exhausted from our long day of travel, walking through an entire mall, and PMS. Yay.

Mom slowly sat down at the opposite end of the couch and just sat there for a little while. I was starting to get pretty anxious, but I didn't really know why. Maybe God was preparing me for what my mom was about to say. She started off by saying, "I need to tell you something." I was 13 at the time, so my mind immediately went to, "Oh no, what did I do now?!" She continued to tell me a little bit more about the abuse she went through during her childhood. I had already known about a good chunk of that, so I was a little curious as to where she was going with her story.

She paused for a split second, closed her eyes, and took a deep breath. When she opened her eyes, I could tell something wasn't right. She looked nervous, sad, and disappointed all at once. Emotions I had never seen from her in that combination before. That's when she told me about her abortions. I could tell she was scared. Scared of what her daughter would think of her. How could she do this? Not once, but twice.

After she finished confessing, she looked back up at me, both of our eyes brimmed with tears. I didn't say anything for a few seconds. All I really remember feeling in that moment was confusion, for sure, but not because of the decisions she made as a teenager. My confusion came from wondering why she felt she couldn't tell me before. I knew abortion was a big thing, but mom had always shown me how to love a person for who they are today - not by the decisions they made in the past.

Because of the example she has always been to me as a mother, and a best friend, I wasn't angry with her. I empathized with her. We all make mistakes, and most of us are too ashamed to confess those mistakes to our loved ones. So when she confessed her decisions to me, I felt closer to her than I ever had before.

Honesty is an amazing thing, and when we are honest with each other, there is a level of respect and love so strong, those things we may have done in the past don't matter anymore. Yes, I had to take a few moments to comprehend all that she had told me. But I knew that without her past, she wouldn't have become the strong, brave woman she is today. She wouldn't have been able to show me what unconditional love truly meant. To love someone unconditionally, you understand their past decisions, but care more about who they are becoming.

So, I encourage you to step up and confess the things that have been holding you back from being the person you know you were created to be. Being a daughter on the receiving end, I can *assure you that I would rather know the things that have shaped my mother to be who she is today. We are closer than ever. There is no gray area in our relationship, and we know that we can be open and honest with each other without any judgment. That is a gift God has given all of us! No, we can't control the answer from the person we confess to, but we can trust that God has a plan. Don't let your past hold you down. Instead, allow it to grow you into the person God created you to be.*

Part 2, Chapter 13
Confession 2.0

It is Thursday morning, and we are driving down I-5 South to Southern California for our first official family vacation. It's the summer of 2010 and the perfect time of year to have a beach vacation. Having grown up by the ocean, I was very excited to take my kids back to my stomping grounds. I was looking forward to sharing with them a piece of my past; where I played volleyball with my friends, places I lived, my first job...think, golden arches. Yah, I rocked the drive-thru.

During our drive down, I was thinking about all the people we were going to meet with when we arrived, and about some of the conversations that might be had and questions that could be posed. One of them is, "Hey Tam, how's your book coming along?" Don't get me wrong, it's not a bad question, except for one thing; my son, Kota, still did not know my story. In fact, he didn't know any of it.

The time had just never felt right to me. He was only 13, same age as his sister when I told her, but telling her was a planned moment. I was very intentional and purposeful in my confession to Kass. I hadn't planned on telling Kota during our big, fun, family vacation.

Kota, much like his sister, was very mature for his age. I mean, his voice was still pretty high, but he reasoned the same as a more mature young man. That always amazed me. He's the same way now. Except for his voice. He had the ability to grasp depth. His spirit of discernment was like nothing I had ever seen before. And, today he still has that same spirit. I swear there were times he knew something was wrong before something really was wrong.

During our second evening of vacation, my boy and I were in the loft winding down a bit. There was a gathering downstairs of our vacation hosts, friends, and other houseguests. Kota and I were putting some clothes in place for morning, getting our beds ready, and sharing small talk with each other. After we had finished fiddling around the loft, we headed downstairs to be with the rest of the group.

On the way down the staircase, it hit me...this is the time. My "perfect opportunity" moment with my son. All the fears that accompanied my heart the day I told Kassidi made their arrival here as I started to sweat and shake as each foot hit a new step. Before reaching the last one, I knew I would have to tell Kota.

Not wanting to risk someone downstairs asking me how the book was coming along, I stop Kota halfway down and ask him to sit for a second. Always willing to have "mom time," he sits right down on the step above mine. He waits patiently for me to say something. His back, leaning against the railing, mine against the wall, we face each other, and I begin...

We had a conversation that he never saw coming. He was surprised to learn his mom had two abortions and was widowed at age 19. His response, "Mom? Are you serious?"

"Yes, I am."

He reached out and gave me the longest, sweetest hug, followed by a kiss on the forehead. I shared a few more details with him and apologized for not telling him sooner. But he understood. He received it so well, like a perfectly respectable young gentleman.

When I told him I thought the book might be titled, "The Day I told my Daughter" he got this big smile on his face and said, "Mom, that is a perfect name for it!" I could see in his eyes that he was proud of me. We talked for a while longer, and then decided to join the others downstairs. On our way down, he leaned over and gave me another hug and kiss, and told me he loved me.

There was something whole about this moment as I realized in my head and heart what had been missing. My husband, daughter, and son are now all on the same page with me. They all know; they all still love me, and they all support me.

Later that evening, the entire house had a spontaneous time of worship with our host, Chad, and Kass on guitars leading us straight to the throne of God. It was then I saw a picture in my mind of my book being completed. I envisioned sharing and speaking to others about my testimony, with my daughter leading worship.

The full circle. The whole story. The picture of grace, mercy and forgiveness for all to see. I don't know if that's just a little daydream or if it'll actually happen one day. All I know is I am now finally ready for it. The main piece of the puzzle is no longer misplaced...

The picture is complete and ready to be shared.

Part 2, Chapter 14
"Dear Dad"

November 13, 2010

Dear Dad,

I learned you were my father when I was seven years old. Mom brought you to our home one night after working a late shift for her second job as a bartender/singer. I was asleep on the couch in the living room where you and mom were talking. Your voices woke me, and I overheard your conversation.

"You know, John, she is your daughter?"

"Yes. I know."

I continued to pretend to sleep, but my heart wanted so badly to jump up, run over to you, hug your neck, and never let go. But, I could tell you didn't want me to know.

It would be another six years before I would hear your voice again. It was my 13th birthday. Mom called me out of my bedroom; she handed me the phone and said, "Someone special would like to talk to you."

"Hello?"

"Hi, Tammy? This is (pause)...I'm your Dad."

I could tell by the tone in your voice you were excited to share this news with me. Although, I had known this for years and had made it my own little secret too, I pretended to be excited...for you.

For the next 13 or so years you'd come around every now and then. You met my oldest child, Kass. She's 16 now. I sent you a birth announcement when Kota was born, 14 years ago. The letter was returned to me..."Moved. Left no Forwarding Address."

Oh, by the way, I'll be 40 tomorrow, on the 14th. I was thinking earlier today about the two abortions I had when I was a kid and wondered, if I had birthed those babies and given them up for adoption, would I want to know about their lives?

I would.

So, I figured you just might want to know about mine. Maybe. Or, perhaps, I just want to share it with you...just in case.

I have a beautiful life. My husband of 19 years is my earth angel. He loves me fiercely, and there isn't a second that goes by that I don't know it.

Our kids...amazing! You'd love them. They're musicians...just like you.

I plan on getting my first book published. It's been a laborious process, but worth every minute.

I'm happy. I'm very happy. Mom taught me to find the funny in every day. Her wisdom has served me well.

I hope you're fine; you should know, you owe me nothing. You've already given me the best gift...life.

So, I just wanted to thank you for the gift of life now, 40 years later.

All the years in between, God, my true Father, has stepped in. He has provided, and shown me more love than I could have ever dreamed of.

My father-in-law has been a dream come true. Yes, I actually used to dream about having a dad. And it came true. He models love and protection on a daily basis.

So, don't worry about me...just in case you were.

I am grateful for my life. And I genuinely hope you are grateful for yours.

Sincerely,
Tam

Part 2, Chapter 15

My Last Goodbye

I learned one April evening while talking on the phone with my mother, that my father had died - two months earlier. She just dropped it in the middle of our conversation. "You know your father died, right?"

Stunned and having no idea what to do with the question, I thought to myself, "Of course I wouldn't know that. I hadn't heard from him since I was 26 when I received back the birth announcement of his new grandson's arrival in the mail with 'Resident Moved. Left No Forwarding Address' written on the front of the unopened envelope."

Along with that memory, came a plethora of emotions, the biggest one being anger. I quickly glossed over her question and continued on as though it was no more important than, "Did you hear that Little Jimmy sprained his ankle?"

"Nope, Mom, hadn't heard. No way I would have." And that was that.

It wasn't like there was a lot of history with him in my life. He left his post very early on. Gone when I was three. Popped back in when I was eight, or so, for a night. Left. Surprised me on my 13th birthday with his, "I'm your Father" confession phone call. He gave me my first life lesson...it's ok to hurt people. But no matter how much his absence, and lack of initiative and attempt to show me love affected me, I just couldn't hurt him back. It wasn't in me.

It is one thing to live life with an absent father. It is another to know for certain there will no longer be a chance for reconciliation.

When I learned on that Saturday night that my dad had died, I had no idea what to do with it. I knew I needed to process this, but my words were a jumbled mess in my head and heart. I think back again to my first childhood memory where I found him hurting my mom. He really hurt me deeply then just as he did when he gave me away at my wedding. He specialized in hurting others. And I know that hurt people hurt people. Perhaps that's what makes me the saddest. Was his heart still full of hurt, regret, and resentment on his last day? I don't know. I will never know.

While that thought makes me sad, I am also a little angry. I am grieving, but not normal grieving. I am not grieving losing him as much as I am grieving the loss of hope to restore any relationship with him. Most of all, I am grieving the fact that I cannot grieve like a daughter should over the death of her father.

I want to mourn him. I want to sit in my tears recalling our first daddy-daughter dance. I want to remember the moment he had to buy me feminine products for the first time. I want to recall the look on his face the first time a boy picked me up at our house for a date. I want to remember back when I was eating ice cream with him on a hot summer day.

I want to, but I can't. All those moments were just fantasies for me.

I wrote him a letter a year ago that was very therapeutic for me. I doubt he ever saw it, but that didn't matter. It was still good for my heart.

So, I will end this with another letter he will never see.

My Last Goodbye

Dad

I am sorry you are no longer here. I am sorry for not trying harder to find you again. Maybe that would've changed things...I just don't know.

I am sorry for the milestones, memories, and moments you missed with my family. I always wondered if you ever thought about us, me, your grandchildren. I thought about you every day. Each day I see Brent with the kids I think about you. I'm sorry you missed so much

I am not sorry that you are my father. I am not sorry that I am here. I am not sorry for your absence in my life...it has taught me so much. It has made me stronger. And though you may have left to hurt me, you likely helped me.

So, thank you. Really...thank you.

I have nothing more to say.

Tam

Part 2, Chapter 16
Welcome To Tennessee

The last time I relocated over the TN state line had been over 20 years ago when I narrowly escaped with my life fleeing back home to Southern California on a three-day Greyhound bus journey. Fast forward to June 2011, I find myself returning to the TN state line once again. Only this time, I'm preparing to make it home.

Just five days earlier, I was on my beloved West Coast standing in my driveway, directing my friends who came over to help our family pack the moving truck. Had you told me 3 months prior to this moment that we would be moving to Tennessee, I would have laughed and laughed and laughed. I had always told Brent that if we ever left Southern Oregon, it would be to move back to Southern California, beach side. But this day, in June of 2011, we loaded every item we owned onto a shady moving truck to trek across the country to settle down in the South. How does that Bible verse go again? We make our plans, but God determines our path? Good one, God! Good one.

I never, ever, thought I would live anywhere besides the left side. And if I were to move, the south was never, ever, on my radar. But there we were, our little family, leaving everything we've ever known to move across the country to work at Cross Point Church in Tennessee. Truth be told, I was pretty thrilled for the change ahead, but equally freaked out. And freaked out for so many reasons.

Our kids were 17 and 14 when we left Southern Oregon. The biggest question we were asked was, "Are they just devastated?!" Well, not exactly. They were thrilled and ready for an adventure by the time we made the decision. Initially, the thought of leaving the city they were born and raised in was tough, especially on our son, Kota. But we decided before we made a final decision to pursue a move, we would take six months and speak nothing of it. We would dig into our lives in Southern Oregon and be fully present in the here and now. We did this so that at the end of the six months if we were still convinced that we were to relocate, then we would continue to pursue the option. We all set personal and family goals to work on for those months while we prayed daily about possibly moving away. In the beginning, Kota would have nothing to do with this move. By the end of the six months, he walked downstairs, looked at me, and asked, "Ok. When are we leaving?" I mean, come on. I just stared at him and thought, "Who is this kid?!" Six months earlier he told us he wasn't budging and would stay and live with Grandma and Grandpa. Today, he's ready to roll.

Within a couple months, we are packing a moving truck and before I knew it I found myself nearing the state line where the state of my life had once been at its lowest.

June 8, 1990, I fled TN. June 13, 2011, just hours from the Tennessee border, it is not lost on me how far I have come. Not only geographically, but emotionally, physically, mentally, and spiritually. Driving my very weighed down car full of suitcases and last minute items that couldn't fit inside the moving truck, with my beautiful daughter, Kassidi, I look over into the right lane where beside us is my husband Brent and our son Kota in the moving truck that almost didn't make it this far. My boys...driving, talking, smiling, occasionally looking over into my car, and making silly faces. Kass is by my side, playing all her favorite music and singing along loudly. My entire being is engulfed in peace. I am not returning as the same person. Instead of entering TN afraid, the way I had left it, I am crossing over into it brand new. If you would have told me all those years ago that I would one day return to the same state I almost lost my life in, I would've laughed in your face and told you that you were out of your mind.

But there I was. Returning. Healed and renewed. There was no way I would have ever seen this coming all those years back. You really don't know what the future holds until you choose to face each day with determination. The many days following my first husband's suicide I was paralyzed. Not even so much out of loss, but out of fear. Fear of knowing I was only 19 years old and already...this. Would this be the picture of my life? Is this what I am to prepare for? Is this it? It couldn't be. I had to find a way out of this mess of a life I was given and helped to create for myself. I had to find the determination to make a change. There was no other choice. No one was going to do it for me. I had to choose change.

Crossing the state line...once again...all I could see around me was change. A husband who adores me; a man in whose arms I know I am completely safe in the folds of. Children who are a blessing from the Lord, of this I cannot deny! The years of struggle, regret, and fear I spent believing that God would take Kass and Kota from me as a punishment for aborting my other two babies. The heart change that has taken place. The lens in which I now choose to see from. Nothing is the same.

It took a lot. It wasn't easy. It was scary and there were countless times I wanted to give up. So many times of defeat where I wanted to run away. It definitely would've been easier to in the moment - but not in the long run. And now here I was, in that "long run."

I catch a glimpse of myself in the rearview mirror. My eyes are filled with tears. Not of regret or fear. But tears of solace, joy and, perhaps, a tinge of disbelief. Is this my life now? Yes. This is my life now. I am safe.

Crossing the state line...

"Tennessee Welcomes You"

I am home.

Part 3

Choose Joy

My response. The following stories are collections of life lesson's.

I don't have all the answers to life's questions, mysteries, or hurts, but God has revealed so much to me on my journey through this life so far. I am not an expert on anything. I am not a counselor. But I am equipped to share with you what I have learned along the way. All I have is my story, and this, my story, I know well. I believe, to the bottom of my toes, that this journey I've been allowed to live has not been in vain. The hurt has purpose. The lessons have value.

I have prayed for you. I have prayed that if any of these words are written for you that you will see them jump off the page and dance their way into your heart.

Part 3, Chapter 1

Victim to Victory

I struggle with the victim mentality. Yes, I know this is a harsh way to start out a chapter, but understand me here. I struggle with this because all too often, it can become an attention-getting scheme that gives a false sense of comfort. However, choosing to remain in this mindset ultimately hurts me most at the end of the day. It's the one thing we have the power to change. To choose well brings power for success. To choose poorly will damage you and those around you.

Choices are a part of life. An empowering reality is to have the freedom to choose. Too often we let this privilege shrivel away for so many reasons. Maybe you're afraid to take the first step and draw a line. Perhaps you believe that living in misery somehow punishes your abuser. You might even believe you deserve to be a victim. For some, it's a badge of honor. For others, it's a neon sign that says, "Don't get too close or try to reason with me...I'm hurting...I'm fragile."

May I make a suggestion? In my experience, the victim mentality will do you no long-term favors. In fact, the opposite will be your reward. You run the risk of stunting your growth. I don't mean physically; I mean emotionally, mentally, and spiritually. You run the risk of alienating yourself and others. Crying wolf will wear thin on the ones who have spent years investing into your well being, only to be rejected time and time again. Listen, that gets old and may lead to trust issues in those around you. My question for you: is all that really worth it?

Not choosing the best action may provide temporary comfort, but that's just it – it's temporary. It will always catch up with us. In my own life, I have found out the hard way that the path from victim to victory hinges on one word...Choose.

Ugh. Let's be honest; it isn't always easy or fun to choose the right thing. It often means we have to spend time and effort investing our hearts and minds into switching gears – gears that might be challenging and uncharted.

Before I came to terms with my past, it was "easy" to do nothing about my hurts. If the fault belonged to someone else, then I always assumed he or she needed to rectify it. Why do I have to walk the hard road to healing on my own? Shouldn't the offenders come to me to apologize and make amends? Don't they owe me? Wouldn't that be fair?

Life isn't always fair.

Yes, I know, when you're in the thick of pain, the last thing you want to hear is how unfair life is from people who seem to have life in perfect order. But trust me, we all have our demons, our secrets, our hurts. Not one of us will get out of this life escaping any type of pain or regret. It's a part of this world, and the result of our freedom to make choices. Which leaves us with two options: live in the thick of hurt as a victim, or live in the thick of victory over the hurt.

Choosing to sit in the past is like hardening cement to the soul, quicksand to the heart. Dig out. The fight is worth it. In spending years dealing with my past, I have learned a few things.

While it is hard to forgive and release offenders, it is one of the most therapeutic, powerful, and freeing choices one can make.

Forgiving does not mean condoning; rather, it is releasing the other person's power over you. "Make allowance for each other's faults, and forgive anyone who offends you. Remember, the Lord forgave you, so you must forgive others." Colossians 3:13 (NLT)

Past memories that often creep into your mind can serve as two powerful tools. Uninvited memories of offenses can be valuable reminders to empathize with others currently struggling to forgive. Also, memories of our poor past decisions can serve as reminders of the person we do not want to be again.

Invite a handful of safe and trusted people to surround you. Get honest and vulnerable before them, and allow them to help you navigate through healing and forgiveness.

Sit quietly with God as often as you can. Just listen. Be still and know He is God...you are not.

Webster defines victory this way, "Achievement of mastery or success in a struggle or endeavor against odds or difficulties."

We all know that this kind of achievement does not happen overnight. This will take time, and it will take much work. It will also require consistency and courage. You will have to allow yourself grace.

Be merciful with yourself, too. Don't beat up your heart because it still wants to ache. It'll have to get used to beating differently. Give it time, but don't give up!

To Choose or Not To Choose

Our days begin with a platter of choices:

Do I hit snooze again?

Is this a dry-shampoo day?

Healthy breakfast or Oreos?

Call that person I've been thinking about?

Blame the dog or don't blame the dog?

Leave the shopping cart in the parking spot or roll it to its "return carts here" home?

Eat in or eat out?

Press the *Like* button on Facebook if I love Jesus?

What to do, what to do?

Whenever my kids go out, I always tell them to make good choices. They usually finish my sentence for me or just say it first proving once again, that all teenagers are smarter than their parents. Of course, until they need their delicates or jerseys washed on the gentle cycle. Who's your mama now?

While life is, indeed, full of options, there are still occasions when we have no choice whatsoever. The fender-bender caused by the other driver. Red lights. Taxes. Unwanted body hair. In-laws. Our neighbor's garden gnomes. I sincerely apologize if you have garden gnomes or are, yourself, a garden gnome. There are just certain things none of us can avoid. With all our might, we try to steer clear of these things but the inevitable wins out.

This brings to mind a time when I lost that battle. And, oh, I was battling. Have you ever come to a moment in your life when you look around at what you've created for yourself and think, "Wow? Is this what I've accomplished? This is it?" I happen to remember the day I asked myself this. I definitely was not happy with what I saw or felt. I had landed in a place so dark and lonely that I had no other choice but just to give up. And by give up, I mean give in, give over, give all, and give way. To give myself permission to let go of the past, hurts, fears, and disappointments, which I had been white knuckling for the majority of my life. I finally arrived at my "enough is enough" moment. My spirit had known it long before my head did, but once my brain figured that out, my heart quickly followed.

The very second this took place, and I kid you not, I instantly began seeing life differently. Yes, I am one of those people. God's Word came to life. You've heard it said a million times how the same Scripture passage read so many times before suddenly becomes very clear. It was true in my case. My husband was no longer a person whom I feared would hurt me like all the others. I looked at my children as gifts instead of "what if God snatches them up for all I have done" threats. I saw around me the people who relentlessly invested in my life. These were my friends and family, those who genuinely loved and cared for me. They could be trusted.

My new eyes changed me. The way in which I viewed life prior to giving in had created a Tam that held everything and everyone at arm's length, and I had pegged them all wrong. No one stood a chance or could break down the barrier that my pain had built around me. It was a very lonely time. And it was sucking the life clear out of me, but I didn't even know it until I was on the other side.

It's amazing how the view changes on the other side. Who knew? Not me. I was too afraid to venture over. Afraid of what? Mostly made up scenarios in my head. A billion "what ifs." At some point, if we truly want to see new possibilities, we will have to choose to be brave enough to reach for them.

Don't Look Back

Do you remember the first time you rode a two-wheel bike? The day when training wheels became a thing of the past; those things only babies used? I can recall my big-girl bike day very well! My training wheels had been removed just days before, and I was riding my bike with the assistance of anyone I could bribe into jogging beside me. I guess you can say I now had human training wheels. I still couldn't ride a bike without someone running alongside, hands gripped to my banana seat as I wobbled en route for the nearest parked car. Nonetheless, those plastic, crooked, rusty old wheels were off, and I was ready for the next step...or so I thought!

It started out a scrape and scab free morning. All I wanted was to jump on my bike hoping this would be the day I would ride all on my own. After several not so subtle manipulating hints, I finally convinced a family friend it was time for my lesson. And with that, we headed out for the drama.

We were off; going back and forth on a little dirt road. Even with him holding on as I peddled my little heart out, I found it difficult to stay balanced. But just knowing he was there provided all the confidence I needed. So off I would go, and he would shout out, "Good job, Tam!" I'd peddle even faster, and my smile would get wider. In no time at all, I felt comfortable enough to start talking to my human set of training wheels as I rode, all at the same time thinking to myself, "I don't know what all the fuss is about – this is so easy!" My confidence was building as I became more positive about my riding abilities and myself.

Then, suddenly in the middle of my spastic chatter, he failed to answer one of my questions. So I asked him again and once more, no response. So, yes I did, I turned my head around to ask him one more time, and he was gone! He was standing at least 100 feet behind with a big smile on his face yelling, "You're doing it, Tam! You're doing it!"

I'm doing it! What am I doing? Wait, you're back there! I'm...OH MY GOSH, I'M DOING IT! Seconds earlier I was cool and assured, but that quickly turned into colossal fear! Then, the predictable happened. As I turned back around to see just where I was headed, I found myself going directly south right onto the dirt road! It was the longest fall of my life, and I fought all the way down until I was weaved in and out like a pretzel in my bike frame. I was scraped from head to toe, well as much scraping as a three mph fall can get you. Either way, it hurt! My deserter came running as I screamed at him, "Why did you let go?" He asked in return, "Why did you look back?"

Well here I am 40+ years later, and not much has changed. Yes, the parallels are jumping off the page! My friend wasn't at fault for letting go of my bike; he knew I was ready. I fell because I took my eyes off the goal and became "scared." I can't even begin counting the times I have looked back and taken my focus off what lies ahead. In many ways, I am still that little girl on a bike. Sometimes I find myself looking behind when I'm in doubt, hoping to find something familiar and common because I'm too afraid of the unknown. And many times, I fall flat on my face.

Lately, I've been meditating on God's omnipresence. The reality of Him existing everywhere at the same time is a lot to grasp, but because I am a believer in His Word I believe everything about Him as well. There are still times when it seems He has stepped out of the room and has left me on my own, but it only feels that way. Certainly, He can't be away from me or out of my presence being omnipresent and all.

So what is it that causes me to feel such a gap or absence? For me, it is almost always a faith issue. What might begin as a strong "bring it on" world expedition can quickly become a personal setback at the first glimpse of disorder. At that point, no feeling seems to be exempt as to how I might respond to the hurdles. That's where my struggle begins. I allow my feelings to dictate my response to adversity. Instead, I should be leaning upon God's Word to guide me. His truths and the knowledge He places in my heart and mind should be my focus, not the sting of fear in that moment.

When I was ready to ride on my own, my friend knew when to let go of my bike. Before that moment, he held on very tight and picked me up each time I became one with the ground. He knew precisely when I was ready to ride off by myself. Even though he released his grip, he was also still there. He wasn't physically attached to my banana seat any longer, but when I turned around I still saw him. I wasn't out of his sight. He stood back and watched me graduate to the next stage. Of course, when it all came crashing down he was there on the spot tending to my self-inflicted wounds and helping me get back on that bike.

I don't know about you, but I still have yet to master balancing life on or off a bike. Thankfully, the Master who holds everything in balance, including me, knows exactly what He's doing! I must trust that when He lets go it's because He knows I'm ready. I must also believe that just because He lets go does not mean He has left me alone, even if it feels that way. Fear and little faith can play vicious mind games, but they can never change the living God.

I am reminded of Peter when he walked on the water

toward Jesus. The second he saw the waves and felt the strong winds he became terrified and began to sink. He shouted, "Save me, Lord!" Jesus immediately reached out and grabbed him and then said to Peter, "You have so little faith. Why did you doubt me?" Peter took his eyes off of Jesus and began focusing on the storm raging around him and down he went. Just like my solo bike ride. I took my eyes off the goal when I feared my surroundings had changed, and down I went!

Today it is essential that I understand my Lord is always – in His omnipresence – right here, right now. When confronting doubting Thomas, Jesus said, "You believe because you have seen me. Blessed are those who believe without seeing Me." Whether I see Him with my eyes or not, it does not change the fact that He is who He says He is! He is an all-knowing, ever-present, loving God who knows precisely what He's doing.

Acts 2:25-26 says, "I see that the Lord is always with me. I will not be shaken for he is right beside me. No wonder my heart is glad, and my tongue shouts his praises! My body rests in hope." (NLT)

This is a promise worth believing!

The Abuse Stops with Me

My daughter will never feel this pain.

Over and over those were the words I repeated in my head. I was 12 years old, hiding in my bedroom closet after taking a beating. Never, ever, will I let my little girl hurt like this!

I had no spiritual influence in my home, yet I always knew there was something more. Hope lived in me...somewhere. Even in the middle of the abuse I would temporarily escape into a safe place in my mind. It's hard to explain now, 30+ years later from that closet moment, but it held me. That one imaginary moment held me in safety even while the belt buckle dug into my flesh...I was alright. And I knew, to the bottom of my toes, the beatings stopped with me. But I didn't break the cycle immediately. I lived several years of life after the childhood abuse perpetuating the pattern through my very own personal poor choices. While flaunting my freedom to do whatever I wanted as a young woman, I still checked in with that guarantee in my gut (knowing now it was God) that I would make it out one day and cut the generational noose.

Eventually, that noose was cut. A lot died with that cutting. Connection to family was the first thing I grieved. I still had contact with them, but it wasn't the same. It really didn't matter much when I began seeing the difference in myself, the change in my desires. All of that happened before I chose to acknowledge God, only later to find He was acknowledging me.

Looking back now I can see it...God was always there with me as He is with anyone, but He never forced His way in. He let me come to a place of choosing. Once I decided enough was enough and my heart began bowing, even before my head caught on, He stepped in. He saw I was willing, and He knew He could work with that willingness.

Choosing is one of the most difficult words in our language to flesh out. Sometimes, choosing good over bad is even more difficult. I am not saying escaping and re-routing a self-dug grave is easy, but it certainly isn't impossible. Often times it's that first step toward a desire to change that can be the catalyst to a new beginning, a clean slate. But you have to want it and choose to choose it.

What change do you need to choose to make?

Part 3, Chapter 5
A Life Saved

Small crowds make me nervous. I feel so vulnerable and visible. Put me in front of hundreds any day! For some reason, that is way less intimidating. But this night, this small crowd was very different. I knew it would be before I even arrived.

It was a small function of women at my church in Oregon where I was asked to give a brief testimony. I chose to speak on the abortions. Trust me, there were plenty of other things I might have chosen; but my Spirit confirmed in me what needed to be said.

The usual greetings and fellowship took place. To be quite honest with you, I wasn't a big fan of women. I had always found them (us) to be catty, competitive, and too insecure and exhausting to be around when there was more than...one of them. So to be in a room with women only was a bit awkward for me. Eventually, I manned up and convinced myself I could do this.

There I stood, center stage, gathering my notes, making small talk with the front row. Making eye contact with the ones I knew well, those who would become my comfort markers if a knee shaking, nauseating moment did happen to arrive.

I introduced myself and shared funny facts about my

family and me. Then I began telling my story when a tall, beautiful woman walked through the back doors. She caught my eye immediately. So very striking. As she made her way to the front row to join her friend, I noticed that she never lifted her head. Her shoulders slumped forward to suggest she really didn't want to be there. I thought...it's a good thing this is a free event!

I continued sharing about my times in the clinic: the pain, the procedures, the regrets, the guilt, the freedom that I came to find, and the forgiveness that God lavished upon me. I shared everything I could in the short time I was given.

I didn't speak for too long - twenty minutes at most. When I wrapped up, in tears, the emcee walked over to give me a rose and prayed for all of us as we closed the evening. As I made my way off stage, I noticed the young woman was already gone. I was hoping to seek her out and meet her.

Two weeks later, on a Sunday morning, I am at church getting ready to join the Music Team for the beginning of the service when I see her, the beautiful tall girl. She came right up to me and asked if we could meet. I was surprised. We hadn't even met. But of course, I said yes. I gave her my number and headed for the stage.

A week passed. No call. A second week passed. Still, no call. Finally, I saw her in church again, but this time I got her number and right then set up a time we could meet.

The day came on a Tuesday morning when she came over to my home. Finally, it was nice to sit and talk with her. There was something about this beautiful tall girl that I was drawn to from the first time I saw her. She sat on my couch, nervous and fidgety. She began telling me her story, not unlike my own. Only, she was currently pregnant. She was engaged with the wedding still months away. Her marriage would give her little girl a daddy for which she was very grateful. But this baby inside her...she didn't want nor was ready for. She didn't want to make the same mistake again of having another baby out of wedlock...a baby that would come before the wedding date. However, her fiancé wanted the baby. He wanted it very much.

She told me she wanted an abortion. She just didn't want another child right then - not that way. She cried and tore a Kleenex tissue into hundreds of shredded pieces while asking for my advice. Honestly, I didn't have to say much. I told her that her seeking me out and meeting together that day meant she already knew what she needed to do. All I was doing was confirming for her what she knew. All she had to do was make the right decision with her heart and mind. After many, many tears and lots of what ifs, she asked if she could use my phone. In fact, there was a little panic in her request as she looked down at her watch. She hurriedly dialed a number as I sat across from her. A few moments later she gave her name to the person on the other end of the line and said she is supposed to be there in an hour, then asked if they would cancel her appointment.

"No," She replied. "I don't need to reschedule."

She handed me the phone and said, "I was going to abort my baby at 11:30 today."

"No, you weren't," I said to her. "I think you had already made that decision before you came today. You just needed a little confirmation."

Her tears flowed uncontrollably. So much pressure, so many questions and fears were bottled up in her heart. She finally got to release them.

We sat and cried for quite some time. In the quietness of my heart, I celebrated the life that was saved. If angels rejoice in Heaven over saved souls, then I'd like to think there was a big celebration happening that day!

Not everyone feels it is necessary to be an open book, but moments like these are why I know I HAVE to be an open book! There is no option for me to be otherwise. A life was saved that day, NOT because of me, but by the redemptive power of the One who saved me. I cannot, and will not, keep that to myself.

Nuggets of Laughter in The Midst of Pain

I was recently listening to a speaker who was spilling out and over with laughter, humor, and joy! I found myself glued to the radio as I drove to get my Vanilla Mocha with whip. In fact, I was so taken by this speaker that once I got to the coffee stand, I had to pull off to the side and put my daily java on hold to finish listening to this hysterical lady. This is what a good laugh will do for me. It will cause me to forget about the things around me - even coffee! All I could manage to do was giggle as I stayed tuned for the next nugget of humor.

I love to laugh. I especially love making others laugh! It just brings me so much joy! As I drove home that morning, with coffee safely in hand, I began considering the effects of laughter. Laughing not only relaxes me, it also strengthen me.

Proverbs 17:22 says, "A cheerful heart is good medicine, but a broken spirit saps a person's strength" (NLT).

Let me ask you a question. Who would you rather be in the company of: a "lemon sucking, woe is me, the world was my oyster, but the dog ate it" kind of individual, or a person who exudes a cheerful heart and whose words are fashioned with joy and good cheer? I know whom I would choose.

In the summer of 2005, I had the joy of being diagnosed with lupus. Yes, I used the word "joy" in that statement. Why do I consider lupus joy? I don't exactly consider the disease itself to be a bowl of cherries, but had the doctor given me the diagnosis while offering me a bowl of cherries...well that might have changed everything. Lupus is not fun, it is often painful, and it daily reminds me that life is temporal. Wow, now I'm starting to sound like the dog ate my oyster.

Several months after being diagnosed, I was going back through some of my journals. I found an entry from a couple of years earlier that took my breath straight out of my lungs. I had asked the Lord to keep transforming me into what He intended. In order for me to be more focused on Him, I asked Him to remove my distractions. And there it was...way back in that request – my answer – the revelation. God was transforming me through lupus. What? How so? Well, lupus makes me weak...truly, literally, weak. Once I thought I was so strong and self-sufficient, but now I realize how feeble and weak I am. I started to focus on God's strength, not on how weak I am without Him, but on how strong I can be with Him.

My father-in-law wrote an amazing book on renewing your mind. Reading his book brought Romans 12:2 to life for me. My thought life had to undergo a huge remodel. "Do not conform any longer to the pattern of this world, but be transformed by the renewing of your mind." My mind needed a re-education. A lifetime of survival of the fittest and fight or flight thinking had to be abandoned. I allowed doubt, and false perceptions to take up residence in my mind. The mind renewing journey was so painful and frustrating (it still is), but only because I white-knuckled my flesh and my "rights" in an attempt to protect myself from others…all habits that grew out of my childhood.

Each day that God allows me to rise to a new morning I tell myself, "I have lupus – lupus doesn't have me."

Better yet, I have a task, and lupus is helping me to accomplish it. This disease has helped me become a stronger and more compassionate person. Because I experience pain daily, I have grown in empathy towards others who struggle with disease and persistent pain. More often I find myself reaching out to others, putting myself in their shoes. Deep down, I know what they're going through.

James 1:2 says, "Dear brothers and sisters (that's me - that's you), when troubles come your way, consider it an opportunity for great joy" (NLT). I can't pretend my life isn't the way it is, but I can embrace the One who has given it to me. He knows my daily struggles.

He's waiting to see how I respond to the struggles of life. Will I let them be an opportunity for joy throughout this entire journey? Or, will I fight tooth and nail while I sap my own strength and the strength of others along the way?

Laughter is one of God's many prescriptions for health. It is a gift, and it is one I enjoy unwrapping and using to its fullest potential.

We all have diseases, and they aren't all physical. We may have the disease of pride, selfishness, insecurity, anger, and all that can infect and ruin our lives. These things can, if we allow them to, dictate our thoughts as well as our actions and responses. Let God transform you. Let. That means it is our choice. It is within us to let God change our thinking and change our lives.

I had the option to allow lupus to change me or to allow God to change me through lupus. I chose the latter. I would never have told you the day I was diagnosed with lupus that I was happy about it, but today, I am very grateful for it. This disease healed me.

Job 2:10 (NLT) [Job says to his wife] "Should we

accept only good things from the hand of God and never anything bad?"

Life is not crippling, but my perspective on life can be. Hebrews 12:12 (TLB) "So take a new grip with your tired hands and stand firm on your shaky legs." I choose to run this race with joy and strength...with no limp!

Part 3, Chapter 7

Why Me?

Do you ever feel alone? Have you ever cried out to the Lord, "Why me?" I'm certain you have a time or two. Does everything you have gone through, or are going through, seem pointless and worthless? Have you ever endured a tough circumstance and wondered about its purpose? Are you still bewildered about it today? Have you ever underestimated your life's experiences and how they may affect other people? Think about this question...have you ever considered it might not be about you at all?

I certainly don't have all the answers to life's tough questions, but I have learned that often times God asks me to endure opposition or hardship for another's benefit. Well, why would He do that? If He wanted to, He could speak directly to that person. Well, He is...through me.

You can have an impact on others through your experiences, and how you share them has the ability to empower others. The integrity in which you share your hurts and how you process them will connect with someone else's hurts. I believe to the bottom of my toes that there is someone on the other side of your healing journey waiting to stand and applaud your courage and give praise to God for His faithfulness. Then, you will have an opportunity to give comfort to them.

2 Corinthians 1:3-4 says, "All praise to God, the Father of our Lord Jesus Christ. God is our merciful Father and the source of all comfort. He comforts us in all our troubles so that we can comfort others. When they are troubled, we will be able to give them the same comfort God has given us" (NLT).

Several times in my life, friends have come to me to say how much God had spoken to them through what I was experiencing. It usually isn't until that moment that I can see what the Lord was doing. All the questioning comes to a stop, and all I'm left with is praise. This brother or sister in Christ needed to hear from or see God in some way, but maybe wasn't quite personally ready to "get it" on his/her own. So God used me. I think about all the complaining and stubbornness that has poured out of me, and in an instant it turns into humility. I realize it is a blessing that God chooses to use and to speak through us. It brings God great honor to count on us to be open and willing. It's then that He can work through us all to reach someone else.

Who am I to think I won't have to endure a little discomfort to be used by God? Jesus endured a lot for me. He certainly didn't have to die a brutal death. He could have escaped it all if He wanted to. He could have walked away and never looked back, but He couldn't get me, or you, out of His mind! He saw the big picture, and though it was for the benefit of the lost, He gave up His rights for us. Those are footsteps to follow.

"You must have the same attitude that Christ Jesus had. Though he was God, he did not think of equality with God as something to cling to. Instead, he gave up his divine privileges; he took the humble position of a slave and was born as a human being. When he appeared in human form, he humbled himself in obedience to God and died a criminal's death on a cross" Philippians 2:5-8 (NLT).

Do not give up. Do not think for one second that your hurts, regrets, fears, and scars are for nothing. They can be the very things that strengthen you beyond anything you've ever imagined and, in turn, strengthen others. I have to remember sometimes not to ask, "Why me?" but to ask, "Who for?"

Part 3, Chapter 8
Burdened

Have you ever been burdened? Of course, you have. Have you ever added to your own burden? Several years ago, I was feeling quite heavy with life's circumstances. My mother had just left our home after having not seen her for over two years. I came down with the stomach flu. Naturally, finances found their way into the burden. At that time, my son was attending a new school nearly 10 miles from home. And I'm begrudgingly trying to wrap my head around the fact my daughter was now in Junior High! You might be thinking, "Ok, what's the big deal here?"

Sure there's more, but I won't share the deeper, heavier stuff with you. And that is my problem and how I add to my burden.

One afternoon, as I was boohooing while washing dishes, the Lord gently asked me, "Tam, why are you so sad? Why haven't you come to Me with everything?" I instantly reverted back to my childhood. I drifted into the small closet I turned into my bedroom so the bad man couldn't find me. My logic was if I can't see him, he couldn't see me. I was safe there. I hid, and I never told of the abuse. As you've read already, I was either a witness to or a recipient of all types of abuse throughout my early years. The last thing I wanted to do was share the abuse with my mother. She had enough to handle herself. I didn't want to add to her burden.

And there it was...my answer to the Lord's question. "I don't want to burden You, Lord!" Immediately, I felt silly, but for the first time I realized why I keep so much bottled up inside! It was a life-learned bad habit and distorted way of thinking. It doesn't matter how I came to think this way. What matters now is I do not have to think that way any longer. And I shouldn't - not as a child of God. His Word tells me to cast all my worries onto Him. He tells me His burden is light.

Matthew 11:28-30 (NLT) – "Then Jesus said, 'Come to me, all of you who are weary and carry heavy burdens, and I will give you rest. Take my yoke upon you. Let me teach you, because I am humble and gentle at heart, and you will find rest for your souls. For my yoke is easy to bear, and the burden I give you is light.'"

Why do I feel so heavy with the burdens of life? Have I turned any of them over to God? No, not totally and completely. Instead, I white knuckle them, and tuck them deep down in the "safe haven" of my thoughts and work solo at fixing all of it. Is this to say I never go to the Lord with anything? No, I'm not saying that. In fact, I take many things to the Lord, but I don't take everything. The "small stuff" is easy to leave with Him. The big mind-bending items, not so easy! I have to stop thinking that God is limited to human capabilities. Furthermore, I must start taking Him at His word! God is my lifeline. But I often try to keep so much of my life out of His line of view.

Even though I came by this self-defeating habit honestly, it does not give me an excuse to continue on living that same way. God expects more from me. It's a matter of growth, obedience, and - most of all - faith. I couldn't trust anyone as a child, but when I met Jesus I instantly leapt from being a child of earthly parents to the child of a Holy Father who can be trusted. Now I just need to start living that truth.

So what do I do with this new revelation in my life? Well, I don't focus on my wrong way of thinking, but I do focus on God's way of thinking, and what He wants for me...to trust Him, surrender, and believe that He is bigger than any of my burdens. When that truth begins to penetrate, saturate, and capture my mind and my heart, it will then manifest itself as child-like faith.

God will really have to have His ears on now!

Part 3, Chapter 9
My Security

Way back before I told anyone about my abortions, I awoke to a day that revealed something huge to me. This day I realized in a very powerful way just who I was and who I wasn't letting go of. My past, as twisted as it seemed, was my security. It was all I knew. My comfort, my "safe" place to land - safe only because of its familiarity, but not safe enough to be out of harm's way.

In spite of this beautiful new life of mine, which included my husband, home and newborn, I was still very attached to whom I used to be. Every day, I carried my little secret with me. It had become a vital part of living. To me removing it would have been equivalent to giving away my lungs; my very breath, something I could not survive without. To let go of my secret would be to let go of me. What a horrifying thought. What would I do? Who would I be?

For many years, I had super long hair that went down to my waist. And, it was permed! Yes, go ahead and guess that decade. When people described me, I was the girl with the "really long hair." That was my identity. It also became my security. I loved people noticing my long locks instead of me. I hid behind it all, until the day when out of the blue, I decided to cut it. I didn't even give myself time to think it over, I just cut it all off!

I didn't know much about the affect my rash decision would mean to me, but I knew I'd be removing a crutch. I cut off my identity and security. I was perfectly aware that it had become my counterfeit comfort. And when it was all gone, I was left with two choices. I could either replace it with something else to hide behind or deal with the issue at hand.

Why was I hiding? What was I hiding from? To be honest with you, I came terribly close to replacing it with an eating disorder I struggled with during my teen years. It would have been simple to invite it back having just had a child and a few extra pounds, which I detested. But upon remembering how tired and sick I constantly felt throughout my journey with anorexia, I chose to pass on round two. Besides, Brent was aware of my struggle with this disorder and would instantly spot its return. There seemed to be nothing for me to latch on to. Believe me, I frantically searched for something. I needed something to be identified by, something that would take the focus off of me. Isn't it funny? I was still putting the focus on me even in my attempts not to.

God's Word tells us that our hope and security are found in Him alone. We have this hope as an anchor for the soul, firm and secure. So now I put my focus on the One who really makes me safe and secure. There is so much freedom in the realization that we are not alone, that we do not have to carry this burden of life solely on our shoulders. Our fears, insecurities, image issues are not hidden from God. They are likely not hidden from others. I don't know where you are in life right now. I don't know what you are holding onto that, ultimately, is holding you down. But I would like to encourage you to consider releasing it. Release it to God, or if that's not your thing, share with someone you can trust and go from there.

Part 3, Chapter 10
Home Improvement

Once upon a time we owned a 980 square-foot home on two acres in Southern Oregon. Our water came from a well, and we had a septic tank, five horses, a donkey and a ghost. I'm not kidding.

The first couple years we invested a ton of blood, sweat, and tears into this place. The kids, friends, and in-laws also joined in on the improvements. It was a family affair. By the time we were done, it looked like a page out of Pottery Barn. We were very pleased with our efforts! But not with the ghost. Again, I'm not kidding.

Brent and I have always loved improving our homes in any way we can. In one house, we repainted the living room so many times I think we lost square footage. It honestly felt as though the walls were beginning to close in on us one layer of whimsical color at a time.

Home improvement is therapeutic for me. I love seeing the change that takes place with a little, and sometimes a lot, of hard work.

Then there's the other home improvement, the "tending to the flesh of the home"…the people part of the home. The spouse, the kids, the cat…maybe not the cat, but definitely the people. Wait…no, the cat, too. But how often do we actually plan on that area of home improvement? Taking inventory of each person, their dreams, fears, calendars, plans? Sharing of your own?

About every 2-3 months, I naturally get a bug to do some home improvement. It usually looks like this:

"Hey, honey? Can we go out tonight? I have some things I want to talk about."

The last time I did this, I came prepared with a list. I was ready to repaint a wall and hammer out some issues. Brent was a nervous wreck. I laugh now, but it was the only way I could keep all my thoughts straight. I laid out some concerns, some ideas, some plans. We tackled the list together, brainstormed, and improved the future of our home over appetizers in downtown Franklin, TN.

While I want my home to be clean, well maintained, and nicely decorated, I desire even more that the hearts of our home be well cared for. What good is it if all my (our) energy is being focused on an image, the aesthetics, the façade? We, as people, are so easily lured in by what we see. You might walk by my home and spot beauty on the outside; you may see pictures online of the new window pane I hung in my kitchen and think it looks fabulous and so organized, or watch a video of our family goofing around in the spotless sunroom. And then, one day, you come over and spend several hours with us. You begin to observe that, while our home is tidy, we are ungrateful and rude to each other. You witness a couple stabbing remarks I make toward my husband. You notice our kids back talking and rolling their eyes at us. And you quickly realize that you were misled by the image we projected, and are disappointed by the reality of our true condition. At the end of the day, what lies true is the state of our hearts. That's what matters most. This is what makes our home beautiful and welcoming. If the inside, the heart, is neglected then no amount of Home Depot receipts will matter. It might look pretty on the outside, but it will feel empty on the inside.

Part 3, Chapter 11
Rejected

Have you ever rejected a gift or a kind word? When Brent and I celebrated our first Christmas together, we were struggling to make ends meet. Our money tree was not sprouting, though our efforts suggested it should be. We both worked hard at full-time jobs and rarely saw each other. We were just starting out and had very little. Needless to say, our first Christmas was financially tight.

Brent and I decided we would set a very small budget, $5.00 a piece, to buy a gift for one another. The next day, on our lunch breaks, Brent headed straight for the mall, and I headed to the Dollar Store! I was practical and bought him things he liked such as gum, Armor-All, a wrench, and a 10 pack of no. 2 pencils with the name "Brett" etched in gold on them (Brent is a very hard name to find).

I paid the damage, went home, wrapped it all up in one box, put a $5.00 bow on top (it's all about the delivery, people), and called it a good venture. As I placed this remarkable gift under our Charlie Brown tree, my eyes immediately bolted to this object lying helplessly alone. My heart went out to it for it had clearly been attacked by a large dose of testosterone. Can we all agree that men do not possess the "wrapping" gene?

It didn't take long to figure out from the outside exactly what it was. It was a Remington wet/dry razor. I'd wanted one forever! And there I sat in a glorious knick-free shaving dreamland until I was interrupted by reality, "I must return this gift!" He went way over our $5.00 budget! Like, 600% over our budget! So I hopped in my car, unwrapped the gift while I drove to...let me see...yes, the price tag is still on it...Sears. With much remorse, I returned the wet/dry razor, and then promptly headed straight to our bank to deposit the money back into our account. I thought I was being so wise and practical.

Brent thought otherwise. I think he was shocked, probably wondering what he had married. Who was this disturbed lady? I'm sure his feelings were hurt and looking back now, I regret that. However, he did learn that I am a low-maintenance kind of girl. Although I require little and I'm not expensive to keep, I do have my quirks. When it comes to buying me a gift, Brent cringes in anticipation of how his ungrateful wife might respond. Poor guy, I should let him do nice things for me. It blesses him when I allow him to.

I think my problem then was that as a child, no gift came without strings attached. If Danny, my mom's boyfriend, did something nice for me, he would expect a favor later. When that happens enough, one might struggle to accept gifts, even if they are given with good intentions and a pure heart. My heart became so conditioned to be on the defense when receiving a gift that I could no longer see a healthy situation for what it was. Even if it was from my new husband, whom I knew was perfectly safe and adored me more than anything.

"It is more joyful to give than to receive" Acts 20:35 (NLT). I need to learn how to accept things from Brent and receive his compliments without a negative retort about myself, or lecturing him on how we can't afford it. It brings him pleasure to do nice things for me, and I shouldn't rob him of the joy of giving.

In time, we got through that debacle. He did forgive

me and accepted our small budget shopping challenge. I think I ended up with some kitchen towels that first Christmas. Now that's practical! In fact, I think I still have them.

It's The Truth

I do not have enough fingers and toes, or other appendages, to count all the times I used to sit in my imaginary world of perfection dreaming of what the perfect life would look like. All the women had perfect Aqua Net-cemented hair. Tang and Ovaltine were free and encouraged at every meal. The Love Boat was canceled. Puberty wasn't embarrassing or uneven. People were nice to each other on purpose. Beatings didn't hurt and were actually a sign of love. All kids passed the President's Fitness test. Wait a minute...what did I say back there?

"Beatings didn't hurt and were actually a sign of love"? Why on earth would I keep abuse in my perfect world? Why would I accept it as normal, or even potentially perfect, and allow it to remain? That makes no sense at all, unless I was convinced I somehow deserved to be hurt and belittled...that my brother and mother deserved it, too. Interesting. So in my young and impressionable mind, beatings were normal and expected. If that were the truth, then I guess there would be no other option than to withstand the abuse. The only way to improve them would be to remove the physical pain, yet not the act. Sounds perfectly logical, right? No!

Let's be honest, hurt will never feel good. That's why

it's called hurt...it hurts. The offender and the offended can spin it all they want in their desperate attempts at justification. One may think they are owed the right to abuse, and the other feels convinced they deserve it. And around and around it goes, the continuous loop of lies. Still, in that loop of lies exists the truth. Truth doesn't just disappear because we refuse to acknowledge it. Neither does it turn its eye away from our realities. It is we who turn our eyes away from the truth. That is what enables us to fabricate and make excuses for our behavior and decisions, but that never removes truth's foundation. We still stand on truth, but easily convince ourselves of being "above" it.

This is how my little girl imagination could run so wild creating that perfect little life. I lied to myself, escaping the truth, to sit in a momentary bubble of relief. Perhaps that is what allowed me initially to forgive my offenders. I turned my eye from what I knew, deep down, was unacceptable; instead, I created reasons why they were all right.

Survival of the fittest was my form of function, which meant that false forgiveness would have to do if only for the temporary relief. It worked in the moment. It's what made it possible for this little girl to skip around in her bruised, swollen, timid, and tattered fairytale life. I needed to skip. That's what little girls were supposed to do.

John 8:32 (NLT) – "You will know the truth and the truth will set you free."

If you're reading this right now and are in an abusive situation, can I please speak to you for a moment? Beings we are talking about truth here – the truth is...you do not deserve to be abused. I don't care how the abuser spins it. You don't deserve it. Period. You never have and you never will. You were not created to be trampled on. You were not created to be belittled. You were not created to be a punching bag. You were not created to be a garbage can for others to hurl insults into. That's the truth.

Some of you may be in a situation where you feel you cannot escape it. If that is you, please find a way to reach out to someone. Please. You deserve more. You deserve your life. The truth is... you have rights. You have been fashioned to live fully. You are loved. You are worth it.

Part 3, Chapter 13
Excuses, Excuses

There was a period in my journey when I justified everything wrong in my life. But whose standards did I use to decide anything was wrong in the first place? Deep down, they were my own standards, and I knew it. Instinctively, I knew better but chose to disregard it. I had as many excuses as there are stars in the sky. Had God not eventually got a hold of me, even now I would be in denial and this wouldn't be a book about redemption. No, it would be a book about excuses and, "How they too can give you a false sense of hope and comfort."

I played the "Pass the Blame game" for a long time. I devoted years to convincing myself, "It's my father's fault. He wasn't there to guide me. How was I to know any better than that?" I finally had to ask myself, how I could convict someone else for my crimes. Why is it always the parents' fault? When does the offender have to shoulder his or her own responsibility? It doesn't matter that my father took absolutely no opportunity to be an influence in my life one way or the other. My choices rested solely upon me.

Then, there was my excuse of when I chose to get abortions... "They offer this procedure, so we don't get ourselves into this mess." That's the kind of mentality that suggests if it weren't okay, it wouldn't be available. Had my life been painted on a canvas, it would have been entirely gray. Yes, did not mean yes, and no, did not mean no. Anything and everything was okay for me as long as it fit into my ideals, and didn't make me the bad guy or feel uncomfortable.

I didn't want to appear to be a bad person, so I made sure no one knew about the abortions. Still, if it hadn't been wrong for me to do it then, I would not have hidden it. There's that instinct again. You do not hide what you are not ashamed of.

Remember when you were a child, and your mom instructed you not to take a cookie from the counter? As soon as she left the kitchen, what would you do? Probably what I did, open the bottom cupboard to use the inside shelf as a makeshift step stool, so I could hoist myself up high enough to reach for a cookie. I would stretch and strain my little arm until at last I grabbed a hold of that forbidden goody. Unfortunately, in the process, I'd knock over the sugar bowl and break its handle clear off. What's the first thing I thought? How can I hide this so mom doesn't find out, or who can I blame for this? To top it off, in all that fear, I'd forgotten to eat the darn cookie! I exhausted myself mentally, physically, and emotionally by never owning up to and taking responsibility for my decisions. And I didn't get to enjoy that forbidden fruit...or goody.

You see, I could go on forever about how so and so never supported me, or how somebody violated me, but they didn't make my decisions. I did. I am responsible for my decisions past, present, and future...no matter what the circumstances may have been or will be. I cannot blame my parents, my childhood, and the bully, or two abortions. I made the decisions; now I must deal with the consequences.

Therefore, I must bear in mind those possibilities. I never considered how the abortions would change the course of my life or the lives of those around me. I can tell you right now that way back then, I never considered the thought that one day I would tell my daughter I had aborted two babies. I would never have admitted then, that I should not have had abortions. I found it too easy when I chose to short circuit two lives.

My abortions were a form of birth control for me. It mattered little. I won't argue over the agonizing position of a family facing a life or death pregnancy. That indeed would be an overwhelming decision to have to make, but I chose abortion because I didn't want a baby. The procedure was easily available, and I willingly accepted it.

One evening our son Dakota, who was seven years old at the time, asked why he had a bedtime. "Why can't I stay up late?" he asked. If we wanted to avoid expanding on this entirely, we could have responded with, "Because we say so." However, there was a lesson to be learned here. 1 Corinthians 6:12 says, "Everything is permissible for me, but not everything is beneficial for me" (NIV).

"Sure son, you could stay up late if you wanted," we suggested. Then we asked, "How do you think you might feel in the morning?"

"Tired," he answered.

"How do you think you would feel at school?" We asked.

"Tired," he answered again.

"So do you think staying up as late as you want would be the best thing for you to do?" We replied.

"No."

You see, just because you're able to do something doesn't mean it's ok. I love licorice and cotton candy! I could eat it at every meal. It's certainly possible for me to do so. Nothing's truly stopping me except that I know it wouldn't be the best thing for my body or health. So, therefore, I choose to eat healthy and indulge occasionally.

The lesson: just because I can do something, doesn't mean I should do it. It takes consistent discipline to make correct choices. It isn't easy or comfortable. It is a constant daily battle for me to remain disciplined in my everyday life. At times, making a right choice means going against the grain. It may not be what everyone else is doing or expecting. You may very well become an outcast. But what is really necessary here? If you have a heart for God, you'll want to seek His perfect will. If so, you'll find yourself in less compromising positions. In any case you may have to choose to do the right thing, seemingly, alone.

Romans 1:18-20 (NLT) says "But God shows his anger from heaven against all sinful, wicked people who push the truth away from themselves. For the truth about God is known to them instinctively. God has put this knowledge in their hearts. From the time the world was created, people have seen the earth and sky and all that God made. They can clearly see his invisible qualities...his eternal power and divine nature. So they have no excuse whatsoever for not knowing God."

It's up to you. It is your choice. If God wanted, He could make us love Him. But even He applies the "permissible and beneficial." Sure, He could force us into loving Him, but all He would get is a bunch of resentful, hard-hearted people. God would be our obligation instead of our passion. His deep desire is for us to come to Him because we want to come to Him.

Part 3, Chapter 14

Stained

Have you ever tried to get a stain out of carpet? Not an easy job! There was a small stain on my carpet in our family room. The first time I noticed it, I attacked it immediately. I got out all the ammo! Those who know me know that I'm a fanatic about clean carpets. My first attempt took care of the stain, and I was very pleased. The unsightly spot was gone.

My achievement even allowed me to reposition the area rug over a few inches where it looked better balanced in the room. Each morning I would walk out and see my big accomplishment and gleam with pride. I got that pesky stain! However, a few weeks later I noticed the spot had suddenly reappeared! Puzzled, I stood there wondering how on earth could that have returned. So I brought out even stronger weapons this time and went to it once again. I scrubbed and scrubbed the surface of that stain, and eventually it went away only to resurface over and over.

This got me thinking about the similarities between a stained carpet and sin in my life. Sin is very much like a stain. It innocently begins like a child with a glass of grape juice walking through the living room. He doesn't intend to spill it on the carpet, but if he is not careful, he will slip and fall and create a stain. I don't seek out sin, but if I am not paying close attention to my surroundings, I, too, will slip and fall, creating a mess. That's when the stain-fighting power kicks into gear. I acknowledge my fumble, do a little scrubbing, tell myself "no" and move on. Then I fall again and again. You know how the story goes.

Why does sin, or that carpet stain, always seem to reappear? It is because our initial efforts to remove the "spot" are usually dealt with only on the surface. To remove that stain on my rug completely, I have to go much deeper than the human eye can see. It would require that I lift up the carpet and work on the padding underneath, the heart and mind, where the stain has soaked in. Until I replace the dirty substance below with something new, the dirt will keep creeping back. What's more is that I would need to do that quickly if I wish not to battle the stain again in the future.

God does not want us to delay. The longer we allow the stains to set, the more they permeate deep within. Did you know the difference between a spot, and a stain is 24 hours? There's some food for thought. Why let it soak in only to battle it over and over again?

Part 3, Chapter 15
Dark Room

Have you ever stared at something for so long that it eventually disappears? I remember as a child being deathly afraid of the dark. Anything that was dark gave me a fright: Hallways, bathrooms, riding in a car at night and especially my dark bedroom. I dreaded getting ready for bed only to have to face my fear of being alone in my dark room. I'd climb into bed and lay there thinking about the scariest or the saddest things I could imagine.

Misery loves company, right?

Just a small bit of light would come from under my closed door where the light from the hallway dimly cast a glow on my carpet. It was pretty, but not comforting. And I would never close my eyes. Anxiously, I'd look around the room until I saw something alarming. Honestly, I would intentionally look for scary stuff. When I'd find it, my eyes would fixate on it, determinedly staring at it as if my life might come to a screeching halt if I looked away. It may come get me if I'm not prepared.

When several, very slow, hours had passed having still not looked away from my imaginary fright, I found that the dark became darker when I looked out of my peripheral vision. The harder I focused, the more I found the dark room matching my obsession. Everything around it would appear completely black. Not even the pretty illumination from the hall light could find its way in. Before long the lack of moisture in my eyes from never blinking would become too much for me to take. I would have to succumb and blink. Just the simple act of blinking shed light back into my room. I actually could see everything after all. Until, of course, I found something else to obsess over.

Isn't that a lot like we are as adults? I have found myself so many times fixating my vision and thoughts on the things of this world, so much so that I lose sight of everything around me. Even good intentions can become total blackouts if not put into proper perspective.

If my focus is always Christ, then there will always be light; but if the occupant of my throne is something self-seeking or of this world, then life will become gray to black. Sometimes all I have to do is "blink" just enough to wake up a little to let the light back in. I made things so complex and unnecessarily frightening and uncomfortable in my dark room when all I had to do was blink and refocus. When I feel compelled to put everything I've got into something that is not of God, or that will not bring Him glory, I'll know. As the things that He has given to me and blessed me with become gray to black, then I will know that I need to clear my eyes, and once again, fix my thoughts back onto Him.

2 Corinthians 4:6 (NLT) – "For God, who said, 'Let there be light in the darkness,' has made this light shine in our hearts so we could know the glory of God that is seen in the face of Jesus Christ."

Part 3, Chapter 16
Own Your Chair

When we lived in Southern Oregon, I was on the worship team. I sang. (I know...who knew.) I've always loved music. Nothing brings me to tears more than the ocean and a well-written piece of music. As much as I enjoyed singing on the team, my real love was writing songs - something I've not done in too many years.

While on the team, I struggled for a long time with being "just" a back-up vocalist. I wanted to be the main show: the one whose voice sang the lead story. Yes, I know, I had a terrible heart and pride issue. I get it. It was ugly; I was ugly. Eww!

Instead of being grateful for the ability, and opportunity to sing harmony, I was resentful for not being skilled enough to sing lead. Icky, Tam...just, icky.

One evening I was watching a PBS show about a live orchestra, and during an intermission the hosts were talking about the "second chairs" and how skillfully they played. And that's when it hit me. I'm second chair. Initially, I was like, why can't I be first chair? My face and heart got all distorted, and I wanted to turn the TV off. Then the show continued, and I began listening very intently to every instrument. Collectively, each chair played its part. Wow...beautiful...heart-stopping!

It occurred to me that first chair needs second chair to play their part and play it well with confidence, with skill, with gratitude, and humility. Without any of these, the first chair suffers. There's no first without a second, and no second without a first. While chairs are labeled, we all still need to work together. One body, many parts. And we must all play our part well. Whatever part we are given, we need to embrace it and know that it is vital to the orchestra's story.

Eventually, my heart got there, and I owned my seat. Today, I love my second chair. I love knowing that first chair needs me to play my part well – whatever part that is. It feels so wonderful knowing that my chair plays a role in the big story of life and I want that role to be played skillfully.

So, to you who may be feeling like your purpose in this life is small or you are not needed...you are. Nothing about your purpose is small or not needed. Your chair is essential to the entire orchestra of life. Your strengths and gifts are invaluable and irreplaceable. Own them and live them well.

Pull up and own your chair. Sit high with confidence knowing that every chair needs the other. You are needed!

Part 3, Chapter 17
Taking a Risk

Growing up I was a scaredy cat. I hated taking risks. Everything scared me: walking to school alone, riding the bus, being called on in class, asking a waitress for water, asking a friend to sleep over. Anything that put me at risk in any way caused me to shy back from everything. I understand a lot of the why behind it all now. I lived in fear for much of my childhood. I was either getting hurt from those who "loved" me or those I loved were getting hurt right in front of my eyes. Life was a risk.

We used to go camping a lot as a family. We would frequent one place often that had a creek running through the campground, or a "crick" as my mother would call it. My older brother and I would play in the creek for hours each day we were there. We'd hop from slippery stone to the next, catching crawdads, splashing each other with algae water, playing hide and seek, being kids, being free without a care in the world. I loved those moments. They didn't seem to come often enough.

During one of our creek expeditions, we came across a drop off. We thought this drop off was created just so both of us could jump off the rocks down into a little pool of water. It was glorious. It was perfect. It was risky. I was barely eight years old, and everything was huge to me. Have you ever gone back to a childhood playground and realize how tiny it is, but all you remember was how ginormous everything was as a kid? The slide was 108 feet high. The swing seat was, at least, six feet off the ground. The see-saw was 1.2 miles wide. Well, I'm sure this little creek drop off was, in fact, little; but to me, it threatened my very livelihood. I couldn't risk shattering my legs jumping off this rock into my impending leg casts. I had sidewalk chalk back home waiting for me to draw hopscotch patterns on the driveway with...couldn't do that with casts on.

But all I could hear was my brother's prepubescent voice yelling at me, "Just JUMP!" Over and over. "Just jump." I'd slowly creep up closer to the edge and quickly step back, stumbling, losing footing on the slimy rocks. I'd get up, rinse off the slime, and try again...just jump! Rinse and repeat. Just jump! Rinse and repeat. I never jumped.

It wasn't for lack of trying. It was the presence of fear. It was the reality that risks were risky and often caused too much pain. My inability to take risks as a child haunted me well into my adult life. I missed several opportunities for growth, discovery, and important next steps. All I ever saw was a cliff - a haunting and daunting cliff. So much of my life had been spent 200 feet from the edge. That was the safe spot...200 feet back. Close enough for me to say I tried but still, close enough for me to say no way! The drop off was too risky. I saw certain pain, disappointment, and a long frightening fall into failure from jumping off of cliffs. Truth is, I never got close enough to see over the edge. The more I stood back, the more my mind's eye crafted worst-case scenarios. Funny, I almost just typed out, "I mastered the fear of taking risks," but then I realized the fear of risking mastered me.

Do you know what I missed out on, what many of us miss out on? Often times the drop off isn't a drop off at all. Our view from 200 feet back leaves too much room for exaggerating the possibilities when there really is only one scenario...the one that waits at the edge. And there's no way to know what that is, unless we walk up to it.

When I would take the risk, do you know what I found most of the time? Just a slight drop off into a beautiful field of discovery and answers. Never the thousand-foot fall I always feared and anticipated. The risk isn't at the cliff's edge...the risk is not walking up to it to see what really is on the other side. The risk is missing out on taking the risk.

Part 3, Chapter 18
Just Keep Digging

No bridge, building, or any structure can stand without a foundation. A foundation's purpose is to support the structure. No foundation, no structure.

Several years ago, while living in Oregon, the Department of Transportation began work on a new overpass near our home. I had to drive through this construction zone every single day, many times a day. There was no alternate route to take, which meant long lines of cars waiting for permission from Mr. Orange Vest to allow three cars through one open lane every 18 minutes. This went on for months and months, and it seemed nothing more was happening...no progress. No noticeable change was taking place at all. No form. No structure. No new overpass to look at...just nothingness. And it started to irritate me.

About four months into this overpass calamity, I happened upon a talk-show radio station while sitting and waiting in my car at the construction site that I grew to despise so deeply. The gentleman began with these words, "The higher you want to go, the deeper you must dig." I instantly knew what he meant, and I immediately applied it to my new-found disdain for this construction zone. I get it! I totally get it! All these months I had been driving on the surface while all those workers were off to the side and far below, digging deeper and deeper so that the new overpass could sit on a sturdy foundation. This would enable the overpass to withstand the weight of all the vehicles that would eventually drive on it. There was a lesson to be learned here. I had been judging and ridiculing these workers for months while they were just doing their job to ensure my safety. When it seemed like there was no progress, and time and taxpayers' money were being wasted, many things were happening below the surface.

As is typical for me, the hard question came, "Tam? How many times have you judged, ridiculed, or talked poorly about others because of what you think you see?" The higher the structure is, the deeper the supports must be for the foundation. I must confess, I have judged many people, friends, and those I don't even personally know who are on their construction journey, solely based on what I see. Instead, they were building and working feverishly below the surface to build a solid foundation.

This makes me think of the many endeavors of mine that have fallen from their shaky existences. I didn't put enough time into them. I invested nothing in the digging process. Perhaps I didn't want to get dirty. Maybe it was too much hard work, or I didn't want to be seen in that horrible construction outfit. But all the laziness, lack of determination, and discipline have only caused more work.

Now, I grab my shovel. And I dig. And I dig. And I dig some more. Are you digging today?

"Each one should be careful how he builds. For no one can lay any foundation other than the one already laid, which is Jesus Christ." 1 Corinthians 3:10b-11 (NIV)

I Built a Wall and It Lied

The same fence that shuts others out shuts you in.
~Bill Copeland

I spent a large part of my life distrusting people. I built a wall around my heart so high and thick that not even the people worthy of my trust could get through.

I felt safe behind my wall because it guarded me against fiery arrows from a loved one's mouth. I was protected from the sting of a blow to the face I might've deserved. It kept me from having to make eye contact with the ones whom I was sure I was letting down.

But you know what? The chamber I sheltered myself with was just false security. The inside of that wall wrote a different story for me to read each and every day; a story that wasn't necessarily accurate but one I chose to absorb for years. The wall told me that no one could ever be trusted again. The wall told me that if I reach out my hand, it would get burned. And just like all the others had said before, the wall repeatedly whispered in my ear that I would never be good enough. The wall said that if I went outside I would get crushed under the expectations of others. Why bother? Stay inside, where you're safe.

The wall…it lied.

While it was me who built that wall, it began evolving into a life of its own...a life full of misery, regret, and shame. And the wall knew that if I gained enough courage to walk beyond it, I would eventually discover all the beauty and truth it had kept me sheltered from. That wasn't safety. That was a slow death.

Funny thing about all this, I lived most of those years behind that wall while "trusting God." In one breath, I declared that God was enough and bigger than my hurts. And I used the other breath to run back behind my wall of security.

I suppose one day I realized that it couldn't be both ways. I don't remember that defining moment, but I do remember slowly choosing to chisel my wall away. Oh, it hurt. It made me sweat. It made me nervous. It made me want to hide indefinitely. But I continued to chisel. One piece at a time until enough bricks had fallen over to reveal what really was on the other side: hope, truth, love, security. They had been there all along, but my vision had been impaired and redefined. By shutting myself in, I shut the truth out. I shut potential out. I shut healing out. I shut safety out. I shut God out.

Sure, God could have knocked down that wall with one flick, but I needed to discover my need to tear down that wall on my own. I learned a lot in my false safety chamber, but I have spent years unlearning most of it. I wish I had scheduled demolition a lot sooner than I did. But this is my journey. And perhaps its purpose is to encourage you to knock down your walls.

Look around you. Are you surrounded by voices telling you that you're not good enough? That you can't be honest with someone? That there is no hope? The voice is your wall. Maybe it's time to knock it down.

Part 3, Chapter 20
Time Heals All Wounds?

As I was putting some of my book chapters together, I was noticing the different timelines weaved throughout my story; timelines filled with regret, shame, forgiveness, pain, and healing. There are portions weighed down with years of shame. Many, many years are packed with regret along with more than an ideal amount of hurt years. The person I am today recalls all of those timelines very well. The sting of each occasionally makes itself known. Even so, my today timeline is laced with healing. No, it's smothered in it. For this, I am very grateful.

The more I reflected, the more I realized that it wasn't just time that healed all those wounds. Although time softens life's blows allowing pain to begin detaching itself from the chambers of our hearts, there is still another big component to healing...effort.

We have heard it said a million times: anything worth achieving is worth the effort. Hurting isn't easier than healing. Effort isn't a walk in the park. It is saying to oneself that I am not going to allow hurt to be my master and the author of my life's timeline. You can spend two years reliving how a person has hurt you, or you can spend those same years releasing their power over you and, perhaps, forgiving them. Most of my healing came through forgiving.

Forgiving is not the same as giving the offender permission to hurt you along with a free pass to get away with it. Rather, forgiving is giving yourself permission to release that burden of unforgiveness so that the person or situation will no longer have any power or control over you. Then you can begin to heal and show grace to others.

Yes, healing hurts, but so does hurt. We don't ignore our finger when we slice it with a knife. We tend to it right away with antiseptic and bandages so that it can begin to heal. We don't just look at it and say, "In time that will take care of itself." Ignoring it will only cause an infection and a much deeper scar. The antiseptic stings when applied but with that effort, it begins to clean out anything that may cause future harm.

Time + Effort.

This is what effort in healing looks like. You experience the initial sting and then you come face to face with the ugly cut. You apply the antiseptic and bandage to prevent infection of the wound. When the day comes to remove the bandage, you may see only a slight evidence of the injury. At this point, it no longer causes pain when touched. When this time comes, you will know you did your part in the healing process.

There is healing in forgiveness. Forgiveness doesn't happen with passing time…it happens because we choose to forgive.

Let this be the day you say, "And now I choose…"

Acknowledgements

Brent - My amazing husband who came alongside me and chose to love me in spite of my past. You have been the perfect model of grace for me. The likes of you was nothing like I knew growing up, but everything I ever dreamed of. I love you so much!

My children, Kassidi and Dakota - You two...you are what mercy looks like. It is because of your lives that I know I serve a very good God! I am the most blessed mom on this earth. You have my heart!

"My PNW Crew" - Your encouragement through the years has been invaluable. Thank you for your love and friendship and for never giving up on me!

Coffee - What can I say...you get me.

Mandy and Jenni - Two of my first online friends who've been my cheerleading team since I first started blogging in 2007. Life is sweeter with you two in it.

To the entire group that helped fund this book!!! Your generosity has blessed me beyond measure. I can't thank you enough!

Thank you to my TN tribe. To all my author friends here who consistently checked on me and graced me with sweet encouragement. My Meaty Monday group! You make Mondays marvelous and my life that much better!

To my In-Laws, Kimball and Lynda Hodge - Wow. The years of patience you have spent on me through this book journey. Each time I'd attempt to throw in the towel, you would catch it mid-air and hand it back to me. You believed in me when I didn't any longer. Thank you for loving me like I was truly your own daughter. Thank you for all the hours you invested into this book to make it what it is today. I love you both so much!

Pete, Jon, Angie, Carlos, Annie, Justin, and Crystal - Your mark on this book means more to me than I can ever describe to you. Thank you a million times.

Daniel White, my photographer and dear friend, you captured everything and more. You are a treasure.

Jesse and Sarah Mae Hoover, could not have done this without you. And, cookies.

Marjorie Poff, for taking a chance on helping to edit this beautiful mess...you are a trooper!

And last but not least - My sister-friend-bestest, Cathi. Being 2,000+ miles away from you gets harder every day. So I should probably thank texting and FaceTime, too. Thank you for showing me genuine beauty and for being my safe place. To the moon...

Made in the USA
Lexington, KY
15 November 2014